PROVOCATIVE ESSAYS IN AFRICAN PHILOSOPHY

Ikechukwu Anthony KANU

authorHOUSE

AuthorHouse™ UK
1663 Liberty Drive
Bloomington, IN 47403 USA
www.authorhouse.co.uk
Phone: UK TFN: 0800 0148641 (Toll Free inside the UK)
*   UK Local: (02) 0369 56322 (+44 20 3695 6322 from outside the UK)*

Published by AuthorHouse 06/17/2022

ISBN: 978-1-6655-9973-3 (sc)
ISBN: 978-1-6655-9972-6 (e)

DEDICATION

Frederick S. Wukari, OSA

CONTRIBUTORS

1. **Prof. Kanu Ikechukwu Anthony, O.S.A,** is a Professor of Religion in the Department of Philosophy and Religious Studies, Tansian University, Umunya.
2. **Ejikemeuwa J. O. NDUBISI, Ph.D.,** Is a lecturer in the Department of Philosophy and Religious Studies, Tansian University, Umunya.
3. **Charles Chukwuemeka Nweke, Ph.D.,** is a lecturer in the Department of Philosophy, Nnamdi Azikiwe University.
4. **Aye, Aondongu Joseph,** is a lecturer in the Department of Philosophy, Veritas University, Abuja.
5. **Paul T. Haaga, Ph.D,** is a lecturer in the Department of Philosophy, Veritas University, Abuja
6. **Onebunne, Jude Ifeanyichukwu, Ph.D,** is a lecturer in the Federal College of Education (Technical) Umunze.
7. **Chinedu Stephen Ifeakor,** is a lecturer in the Department of Philosophy, Nnamdi Azikiwe University, Awka.
8. **Philip Osarobu ISANBOR,** is a lecturer at St Albert Institute for Higher Education Fayit-Fadan, Kagoma
9. **Peace I. Osaghae,** is a lecturer in the Department of Philosophy, Veritas University, Abuja.
10. **Ufearoh, Anthony, Ph.D,** is a lecturer in the Department of Philosophy, University of Calabar, Calabar.
11. **Ejike, Emeka Cyril**, is a lecturer in the Department of Philosophy, Nnamdi Azikiwe University, Awka.
12. **Aghamelu Fidelis Chuka,** is a lecturer in the Department of Philosophy, Nnamdi Azikiwe University, Awka.

TABLE OF CONTENTS

INTRODUCTION

The present work is a collection of papers that border on the African philosophical enterprise. And these papers address fundamental questions and clarify crucial concepts in the area of African philosophy. The first chapter addresses the questions: Is there anything like African Logic? If yes, what is the nature of African Logic? It employs the philosophical method of analysis to argue that there is African Logic. It maintains that an organized life, like that of the African people, cannot be possible without the tool of logic that is anchored on the culture of the people. It established that African Logic is a major branch of African Philosophy which deals with the thought-pattern, language and worldviews of the African in the African world. The second chapter, using Levinas' philosophy looks into the phenomenology of Otherness, unlike the capitalist perspective that sees the other in terms of profit and loss, it calls for a communalist understanding of the other as a co-traveler in the project of African development. Chapter three ventures into the Tiv conception of immortality, which has received little attention from scholars especially that of Tiv extraction.

The fourth chapter evaluates the theories and conceptions put forward by scholars in their bid to evolving a promising non anthropocentric African environmentalism. While the fifth chapter focuses on a metaphysical and epistemological study of African Medical Practitioners, the sixth chapter discusses African Epistemology. Chapter seven addresses the major methodological problems in Nigerian democratic structure and demonstrated the nexus between freedom and democracy. The eighth chapter gives a clear meaning to political globalism in Africa, its importance and effects on African political growth. Chapter nine stands for the thriving of religious pluralism with its ingredients of religious freedom and respect for human rights and dignity against the weighty negative effects of religious fanaticism and fundamentalism. While chapter ten takes the reader back to the issue of Africa and globalization, chapter eleven discusses Fanon's political philosophy of revolution. The work closes with a chapter on the dynamics of individuality and communality in African ontology.

This work titled: Provocative Essays in African Philosophy has provided the desired atmosphere for African philosophers and philosophically inclined writers from various disciplines to bring their distinctive methods to bear on problems that concern everyone. This work is, therefore, strongly recommended for all who treasure good philosophical literature; and most especially for anyone who wishes to be abreast with important debates and developments in African philosophy.

Experts, researchers, undergraduate and post-graduate students, beginners and casual readers in the area of African philosophy are bound to treasure the usefulness of this piece.

Prof. Kanu Ikechukwu Anthony, O.S.A
Department of Philosophy and Religious Studies
Tansian University, Umunya

CHAPTER ONE

AFRICAN LOGIC

Ejikemeuwa J. O. NDUBISI, Ph.D.

Executive Summary

As a major branch of philosophy, logic deals with the basic principles, techniques and methods for distinguishing good arguments from bad arguments. It focuses on the validity and/or the soundness of our reasoning processes. It is through the instrumentality of logic that we can distinguish between truth and falsity, consistency and inconsistency, validity and invalidity, etc. in our daily usage of language. Logic is a prerogative of the human person as a rational being. However, some scholars have argued for the non-existence of African Logic. This position has troubled the mind of the researcher. The pertinent questions now are: Is there anything like African Logic? If yes, what is the nature of African Logic? Therefore, employing the philosophical method of analysis, this study strongly argues that there is African Logic. It maintains that an organized life, like that of the African people, cannot be possible without the tool of logic that is anchored on the culture of the people. This study finally submits that African Logic is a major branch of African Philosophy which deals with the thought-pattern, language and worldviews of the African in the African world.

Keywords: Logic, Philosophy, African logic, African Philosophy, Rationality

Introduction

The word logic is not new to many of us. We have heard of it before and many of us have used it severally in our speeches and writings. But despite its familiarity, it is a word that most people find difficult to define in clear terms. This is because the word 'logic' can be used in several senses. Francis Offor identifies three major ways in which one can look at the term 'logic' all of which are equally correct. In the first sense, the term logic is used to describe the totality of all laws guiding the human thought (Offor, 2010, p.3). It is a truism that humans are rational beings whose thinking processes are based on certain principles. The totality of these principles can be described using the word 'logic.'

In another sense, the word 'logic' can be used to describe the principles guiding the operation of a mechanism. Every gadget or thing has its own inner logic which describes the way such a gadget or a particular thing operates. For instance, when we operate our GSM handset, it follows a given procedure. When a call comes in, we have to press the 'receive' button and the call is received, and to end the call, we have to press the 'end' button. If we press the 'end' button and the handset starts sending messages indiscriminately, then something is wrong and the set will be said not to be operating the way it ought to, that is, according to its inner logic. Therefore, the operation of a mechanism is guided by certain principles which can be referred to as the inner 'logic' of that mechanism.

The foregoing conceptions of logic are all correct in their own right, but these are not usually the ways in which professional logicians speak of logic. They often speak of logic in its strict and technical sense as an academic discipline. In this sense, logic is therefore seen as that branch of philosophy that deals with the study of the basic principles, techniques, or methods for evaluating arguments (Bello, 2000, p. 1; Offor, 2012, p.3; Ndubisi, 2014, p. 32). Understood in this sense, logic reflects upon the nature of thinking itself; it attempts to answer such questions as: what is correct reasoning? What distinguishes a good argument from a bad one? Are there methods or ways to detect fallacies in reasoning, and if so, what are they? Indeed, this project of discerning between correct and incorrect reasoning is the central problem with which logic deals and all the principles and techniques in the logic of any people are developed primarily for the purpose of this discernment.

Now we have seen that logic can be used in more than one sense when it is looked at in its loose, technical, professional and academic senses. Offor, (2010, p.2) describes logic as a branch of philosophy that teaches us the basic principles, techniques and procedures for distinguishing good arguments from bad ones. This is in line with Copi who defines logic as the study of the methods and principles used to distinguish good (correct) from bad (incorrect) reasoning (Copi 1994, cited in Jaja&Badey, 2012, p.96). By correct reasoning, we mean the art of finding reasons and/or evidence which do, in fact, support and /or prove our conclusion (Ndubisi, 2014, p.32). Echukwube provides a rather instructive definition of logic when he states that logic is concerned with the process of thinking and reasoning as well as the symbolic expression of such process in verbal or written form (Echukwubeas cited in Jaja&Badey, 2012, p.96).From here, one can understand logic to be science of reasoning by which problems are solved and conclusions drawn from premises. In fact, one is said to be engaged in logic when one reflects on and examines the principles in terms of which understanding and right judgment must be achieved. Hence, Aja (2008) maintains that logic is interested in justification of ideas and assertions (p. 3). Copi (1982) emphatically averred that logic studies the method and principles by which we differentiate good reasoning from bad reasoning and correct reasoning from incorrect reasoning (p. 21).

Logic concerns itself with the proper method of reasoning, for the art of sound, correct and critical reasoning is in the domain of logic (Ndubisi, 2014, p.32). Logic distinguishes between truth and falsity, consistency and inconsistency, orderliness and disorderliness, validity and invalidity in our daily approach to reality by use of language. As I have noted elsewhere, it is the function of logic to dispel the confusion that often arises in our everyday discourse and, indeed, the human person is called rational on the ground of his natural ability to engage in logic (Ndubisi, 2014, p. 32).

Logic: Universal And Cultural

Logic is a branch, a tool, and the most rigorous aspect of philosophy. As Ogugua and Ogugua (2015, p.244) observe, and rightly too, it lies at the core of philosophy. As a tool of philosophy, logic looks like philosophy in so many ways and we cannot truly engage in philosophy without it. Like philosophy, logic is both bound and boundless; both universal and cultural. Let us first highlight the fact that philosophy has these characteristics.Philosophy could be viewed from different perspectives. Etymologically, its definition stands to be love of wisdom. It can also be seen as a people's worldview or an attitude towards life. All these point to the fact that philosophy is both a universal enterprise as well as an enterprise within the bounds of culture. Philosophy as an enterprise is not necessarily academic. Thus, Ogugua and Ogugua (2015) aver that it is a many sided enterprise with degrees of ascension and acceleration in the journey of thought, wonder and meditation (p.244). This is not particular to philosophy alone. The academic and non-academic aspects abound in other disciplines and human enterprises including religion, mathematics, science, etc. We do find people ordinarily called illiterates doing well in mathematics and medicine. These are not 'academic' mathematics or medicine, nevertheless they are mathematics and medicine and there is no need to tag them 'debased' as most purists of our time do. Therefore, it will be expecting too much from every people to have at once philosophy that is purely academic or theoretic. This is because philosophy has always grown out of a people's understanding of the meaning of realities in their worldview.

Without the culture of a people, therefore, philosophy is almost impossible. Philosophy results in a place only when people of/in a place attempts to arrest the challenges and problems of that milieu through critical thinking. What we know today as African Philosophy is a product of African trying to understand the realities in the African world through rational means. Understood in this sense, philosophy inasmuch as it is boundless by reason of its universality, is equally bounded by cultural influence, and this is why we can rightly speak of African, Chinese, Indian, British or American philosophy. What this suggests is that although philosophy is universal, it is not boundless. There are boundaries, because every people will undertake the quest for understanding the meaning of realities and human existence differently in accordance with their different worldviews.

But if philosophy is truly relative in this sense, as we have already made clear, then logic too is affected notwithstanding that logic is, as Ogugua and Ogugua puts it, a science of pure form. Logic too has universal and cultural elements. Its universality lies in its form (artificial logic), while natural logic is culturally bound. This point is well highlighted by Ogugua and Ogugua (2015) when they observed:

> Logic does not pay attention to either truth or matter or declarative sentences as such but one would expect the difference to lie in and with natural logic and not with artificial logic. It will be out of place for one to expect Igbo-African logic to be at the level of sophistication as the formalization and abstraction of thoughts, making the study of forms in logic removed from the realities of thought and language; that is, being myopic as to suffer from mania for symbols. (p.244)

The fact is that knowledge of artificial logic is only acquired in the class room. But it is absurd to say that uneducated people or even those who have not taken any course in neither philosophy nor logic does not apply logic in their life experiences. This means that the universal, abstract or artificial logic, that is, thestudy of forms, is not all there is to logic. Yes, logic can be universalized because it has to do with symbolization, but there is more to logic than symbols. The idea of logic shows that it is not out of place to have African logic – a sound logic concerning itself to matters of practical import – a logic serving the purpose of language, law, morality, habit etc – a tool for articulation, appreciation, and understanding realities in Africa (Ogugua&Ogugua, 2015, p.244).

There is Western logic and there is African logic. There is logic in all cultures inasmuch as there is language through which they attempt to understand and explain reality.

Is there an African Logic?

From the discussion above, it is clear that an organized life, a way of life cannot be possible among a people without the tool of logic. How could a people deprived of logic have a culture including language? How could they achieve right reasoning as rational beings? In fact, how could their lives be meaningful? Logic is concerned with the clarification of language and it facilitates correct reasoning. Generally, it ensures that one has an ordered facility. It is clear that without logic, it is practically impossible for one to perform basic human functions including linguistic functions. This is premised on the fact that the capacity to organize reality intelligibly by means of language is made possible by logic.

The truth is that without language, life itself will be meaningless. Logic is central to any culture because every culture has a language and language is only made possible by logic. Every language belongs to a culture and every culture belongs to a people. Logic makes language possible, and language expresses culture. It follows therefore that culture presupposes the existence of logic. On account of this connection, one would discover without much ado that logic is fundamental to African worldview. This is why we make bold to assert that logic is an element of culture. Africa as a whole has a culture, and all of its parts are embellished with cultures, all of which can only be possible with logic. The logic inherent in any given culture is made more manifest by the language of the people. For this reason,Ogugua&Ogugua (2015, p.247) aver that the logic of a people is not only discernible but discoverable in their language. And it is in respect with the logic found in a people's language and behavior that we postulate the existence of African logic.

Logic can have no content and form without language, and language is used to express or picture reality. Therefore, logic has to do with the way we speak about things, about what is. But a discourse of what is, is a metaphysical discourse. Metaphysics is the study of whatever is insofar as it is – the study of being. The study of being, however, is not exclusive to Metaphysics. Epistemology, properly understood, is also a study of being from quite a different perspective. Metaphysics studies being from the point of view of existence while epistemology studies being from the point of view of cognition. The study of being, however, primarily belongs to Metaphysics because Epistemology does not enjoy unlimited scope that Metaphysics enjoys: what is may not be known or even knowable. But we do not have the logic to speak of what is not known to us. Logic as an epistemological tool only furnishes us with wherewithal to talk about reality as we encounter them. It is right then to say that epistemology is an instrument of Metaphysics itself mainly concerned with ontology, while logic is that of Epistemology.

I have highlighted this inevitable connection between logic and epistemology elsewhere when I noted that:

> Epistemology inquires into the nature, possibility and veracity of human knowledge. It deals with the object and problems of human knowledge. Logic, on its part, distinguishes correct reasoning from incorrect reasoning. It borders on the criteria or the yardstick for our acclaimed knowledge...Logic provides the necessary 'instruments' for proper presentation of what we claim to know. (Ndubisi, 2014, p.32)

Now the objects of our knowledge are beings, things, what is, and not no-thing. Epistemology makes use of logic to venture into reality and experience has shown that the whole of the human race does not view reality from a common perspective. We often do not fix attention in the same object during cognition and even if it so happens that we do, each of us looks at it from his or her perspective. So, the answer to the question of the existence of African logic is very clear. Without going into the Great Debate on the Existence Question of African Philosophy, we note that the fact that there exists African Philosophy, presupposes the existence of African Logic. Thus, Kanu (2017) avers that, having established the existence of African philosophy, it would be illogical and contradictory to ask the question: is there an African Logic. Uduma (2015) observed that:

> The existence of African Philosophy is supposed to dovetail the existence of an African logic. So even if we cannot currently present one, the possibility should exist. After all, African philosophy itself is relatively very recent and to overcome the tension that governed its emergency its corollary African logic should be accepted even if it is only conceptually (pp. 59 – 60).

Indeed, no group could have existed for any length of time without the ability to reason and think, that is, without philosophy. Furthermore, man's ability to make use of language undoubtedly presupposes the presence of a fundamental logical disposition. In this regard, Africa is not an exception.

The Concept and Nature of African Logic

Jaja and Badey (2012) define African logic as "the application of the thinking process on the African world, language, culture and objects" (p.96) . For them, although the African logic is natural, it allows the artificial symbolic logic of the West to influence it. By natural logic is meant critical, discriminating, rational and reasonable discussion and discourse in natural language, and by artificial logic is meant the setting up of constants, variables, sentence connectives and deduction and transformation of rules, for deriving the formal validity of arguments and symbolic logic (Momoh, 1989, p.167). Logic precisely is that pattern of thought found in everyday discourse of a people (Jaja&Badey, 2012, p.96). It is concerned with the clarity of expression, the avoidance of fallacies, vagueness, ambiguity and contradictions in language.

Thinking and reasoning is not peculiar to any particular people even if we grant, and we think this is true, that, not every thinking is reasoning. We may think of so many things even as we carry out our daily tasks or listening to a speaker in a gathering without really applying our reasoning to them. This attitude in human cognition also applies to all humans as does the application of logic to facts of life. Reasoning is the activity or process of adducing, collecting evidence, weighing them, and drawing conclusions based upon these evidences (Ndubisi, 2014, p.32).

African Logic is a major branch of African philosophy and it deals precisely with the application of reasoning to the world and culture of the African, to his language and object of his reference. Thus, Jaja and Badey (2012, p.96) observe that African logic deals with thinking [understood as reflection, assessment or reasoning], language or inference all of which are usually with reference to one's world and culture. Since language is the tool of the philosopher, African language becomes the vehicle of African logic.

African logic is shaped therefore by the way the Africans view reality. It is a natural logic encompassing the entire worldview of the African peoples and culture. African logic thus concerns itself not so much with abstract reasoning as with difficulties and problems of real life. This is why Jaja and Badey (2012) are of the view that African logic is that natural logic which applies to juridical, pragmatic and concrete problems in the African existential world (p.101). Thus, the African logic is not satisfied with mere validity of arguments. Emphasis is laid on the truthfulness of each claim.

The African logic from what we have said above is connected to their ordinary language. As already noted, language would be an unrealistic dream without logic. Nevertheless, the rules, principles and laws of logic are quite evident in African mode of thought. Indeed, there is no doubt that the ordinary language may not be able to be used in making subtle analysis and distinctions. This reason, observed, Ogugua and Ogugua (2015, p.248), compels some thinkers to hold that symbolic logic with its artificial logic is of prime importance.

The artificial language of symbolic logic appears more perfect than the natural language to some philosophers. Hence, some philosophers try to formulate their theories in such artificially regulated logistic language (Unah, 1998). We do not attempt to deny the scientific nature and value of the artificial or symbolic logic, but we do not think that it is a *condition sine qua non* to logical thinking nor is it the very essence of logic generally. As a matter of fact, the essential characteristics of logic can be realized by the use of natural language, symbolism standing only for elegance and precision.

It is true that natural language has the tendency to accommodate vagueness. This point notwithstanding, logic in its natural language is nonetheless logic, also embodying completeness of thought. The African logic does not have to be subject to logical calculi to be called logic. This is not to say that our thoughts cannot be formalized or symbolized painstakingly. Of course that is possible. But there is nowhere that an individual is subjected to logical calculi to show that he/she is logical; not even in Europe.

Actually, one has to be a logician in the academic sense or a philosopher to truly understand the mathematical logic. The fact is that the Traditional European cannot understand mathematical logic without proper training. Logical ability restricted to formal truth in logic is, without doubt, a monopoly of trained logicians, not even trained philosophers (Ogugua&Ogugua, 2015, p.249). Therefore, the African logic is essentially logic in natural language and no one would dare to deny without contradictions that this is logic. It is a logic observing the syntactical and semantical rules and the rule of right inference and of valid argument though the Africans did not set out these rules in form of mathematical symbols. The fact, then, that the Africans have logic is clear from the fact that they have always made inferences in life and have always seen nature or reality as something intelligible, and indeed, they have organized reality in history. This is what Levy Bruhl failed to understand when engulfed in the darkness of prejudice and the desire for White superiority he asserts that the Africans are pre-logical, primitive and lacking in logic. Holding this sort of view is the very height of ignorance (of the nature and dimension of logic), for logic remains the intellectual sheet anchor of a people's appreciation of life.

Conclusion

History, learning and experience show that the Africans are logical in their thought and behavior. This could not be possible if there is not in Africa the existence of logic. There is no gainsaying the fact that the Africans know and recognize what is now known as the laws of thought namely, law of identity, law of non-contradiction, and law of excluded middle. These laws are seen in operation when the Africans make attempts to resolve their day-to-day problems. Here, one finds out that the African knows that what is is, and what is not is not; and that something cannot *be* and *not be* at the same time for this entails inconsistencies. They do this without necessarily having to pattern their thought in the formal structure of syllogistic logic or engage in prepositional logic – and we do not think we learnt from any other people to do this even if any other people does so. African logic is therefore an existential reality.

> Logic as we have elaborated is a concern with correctness of argumentation. Once we identify the subject matter of logic as arguments, it becomes clear that logic lies at the heart of human existence; human life is directed by argumentation. This

applies to the African as it applies to all cultures. Arguments thus mean reasoning and the African's ability to conduct his daily affairs ordinarily means that he is eminently logical (Uduma, 2015, p. 67).

In sum, there is African logic which deals with the thought-pattern, language and worldviews of the African in the African world. The works of many African philosophers, in this regard, attest to the existence of African logic.

References

Aja, E. (2008). *Logic and Clear Thought: An Invitation to good reasoning, 2nd ed.* Enugu: University of Nigeria Press.

Bello, A. (2000). *Introduction to Logic.* Ibadan: University Press.

Copi, I, M. (1982). *Introduction to Symbolic Logic.* New York: Macmillan

Jaja, J.M. and Badey, P. P. (2012). "Logic in African philosophy: Examples from Two Niger-Delta Societies" *International Journal of Academic Research in Business and Social sciences, 2(4). Pp.* 95-102.

Kanu, I. A. (2017). Igwebuike and the Logic (Nka) of African Philosophy. *IGWEBUIKE: An African Journal of Arts and Humanities. 3. 1. 9-18.*

Momoh, C.S. (1989). *The Substance of African Philosophy.* Auchi: African Philosophy Projects' Publications.

Ndubisi, E. J.O. (2014). "Nature and function of logic in African epistemology" *International Organization for Scientific Research Journal of Humanities and Social Science,* 19 (11) Pp. 32 – 36.

Offor, F. (2010). *Essentials of Logic.* Ibadan: Book Wright Nigeria Publishers.

Ogugua, P.I. and Ogugua, I.C. (2015). "Is there an Igbo African logic?" *Open Journal of Philosophy,* 5, Pp. 243-251.

Uduma, U. O. (2015). "Beyond Irredentism and Jingoism: Reflections on the Nature of Logic and the Quest for (an) African Logic". [7th Ebonyi State University Inaugural Lecture].

Unah, O. (1998). "Logic as an Element of Culture". In Unah, J. (ed.) *Metaphysics, Phenomenology and African Philosophy.* Ibadan: Hope Publications. Pp. 374 – 391.

CHAPTER TWO

EMMANUEL LEVINAS' CONCEPT OF OTHERNESS AND THE AFRICAN EXISTENTIAL SITUATION: A HERMENEUTIC ENGAGEMENT

Charles Chukwuemeka Nweke

Executive Summary

This paper attempts an interpretation of African existential situation in the light of Emmanuel Levinas' theory of the Other. The paper presents that the bid to find measures towards the advancement of humanity forms a very vital concern of philosophy. Thus, several efforts have been made by philosophers over the ages to multiply viable options which are considered by various world societies as veritable tools for their socio-political advancement. When compared with the technologically driven Western society, Africa still struggles to measure up with global defined development with all negativities attendant of such situation. Notably, the works of many philosophers are not only the products of their intellectual curiosity but sometimes informed by their experiences in life. Thus, informed by his life experiences, Levinas delved into a phenomenology of Otherness in which he postulates an ethico-political theory aimed at the need for the of universal care of humanity, a theory which the paper considers a veritable hermeneutic tool for rethinking African existential situation. Africa's rise in the global developmental scene, the paper finds, requires basically the eschew of viewing the other(Africa) by another(West) as an object of capitalist exploits, but a communalist co-traveler in the project of African upliftment cum global development.

Introduction

The quest for the preservation of mankind assumes various dimensions at different epochs of human history. The Hobbesian imaginary postulation of man's transition from the state of nature to civil society projects man's innate desire for survival in a situation of chaos and anarchy. As the human society evolves in its diversity, so does history harbor the attendant developmental steps of nations. The scientific revolution and advancement of the modern period lifted the Western world to the height of development leaving the rest of the world including Africa at the threshold of either under-developed or developing world. As the developed world is relatively at home with existence, Africa is regrettably still struggling with the rudiments of life and seems irremediable in its perilous conditions. Thus, African existential situation is pitiable.

Nevertheless, any viable discourse on the African condition ought to take into cognizance the factors that contributed to and still sustain the predicament. The bid to respond to the situation takes the present project to co-opting Levinas' concept of otherness which advocates for fairness and objective care of the other as a necessary condition for the utmost advancement of the human society in general. When the Western colonialism is considered in the light of Levinas' concept of otherness, the Western colonization of Africa remains condemnable in its exploitative tendencies. The theory is equally a veritable tool for conscientize the West on the negative implications of imperialism, neo-colonialism and globalization. Thus, an ethically based international liaison should be geared towards the integral development of nations for the sole purpose of universal common good.

This paper of three sections therefore adopts a hermeneutic approach in its bid to rethink the African existential situation in the light of Levinas' concept of otherness. The first section will be a concise articulation of Levinas' concept of otherness. In the second section, the African existential situation will be widely exposed. The last section will display the hermeneutic significance of the piece in the bid to re-thinking the African Existential situation in the light of Levinas' concept of otherness.

Levinas' Concept Of Otherness

Levinas' idea of otherness finds expression in his notion of ethics as the first basis of philosophy whereby "the other is not knowable and cannot be made into an object of the self." (Wikipedia) Rather, "the other reveals himself in his alterity not in shock negating the I, but as the primordial phenomenon of gentleness." (Routledge Encyclopedia of Philosophy, 1998) Levinas' intention was to project a progressive intellectual revolution in philosophy after the trend of the analytic philosophers, although informed by the circumstance of his time.

Hence, Levinas launched an ideological attack on traditional metaphysics (ontology) accusing it of making 'the other' an object of subjectivity. According to Levinas, philosophy cannot be "love of wisdom", for that relegates the care of the other and seeks self gratification (knowledge). Rather, philosophy should best be defined as "wisdom of love" (ethics) where the otherness of the other is upheld as a natural obligation, locatable with reason. Consequently, ethics is first philosophy since the traditional philosophical endeavor of knowledge is but a secondary feature of a more basic ethical duty to the other.

In *Totality and Infinity*, Levinas maintains that the other human being in his separation calls me into question. What this entails is that the care of the other is a matter of ethical obligation. Hence, "in the face-to-face relation, my self-assurance disappears and I find myself in bad conscience"[3]. This instance presupposes an unlimited and committed obligation to the other. Levinas, thus, denies the conception of ethics in terms of intension or legal responsibility since those are artificial. Hence, justice as the reciprocal system of obligation is not in accord with reason. Rather, as "the I is questioned by the other within the face-to-face relation, so justice is put in question by the face of the other" (Ibid)

In Levinas' ideal, the other is the sole determinant of personality and identity in so far as the other reserves the prerogative of questioning the identity of the I. As such, to be is to be for the other. And to be for the other is to be without identity since in the other the identity of the I is substituted. With this formula, the I is an other. His *Otherwise than Being* reflects Levinas' effort to portray "the substitution of the I, whereby subjectivity is being hostage."(Ibid, 581) Consequently, subjectivity is not the ego isolation of modern philosophy, but the restlessness of being disturbed as a result of the concern for the other.

For Levinas, the irreducible relation, the epiphany, of face-to-face, the encounter with another, is a privileged phenomenon in which the other person's proximity and distance are both strongly felt. Such encounter produces a revelation that makes a demand to affirm and express the other's freedom. Consequently, the transcendence and heteronomy of the other is recognized and upheld.

African Existential Situation

The term 'African Existential Situation' (AES) refers to the condition of the African world considered from the political, social and economic dimensions. It equally comprises of both real and imagined perspectives on the continent Africa. In the global development prism, Africa is branded a third world with all notable stigma attached to such placement. For instance, questions abound as to the authenticity and tenability of the term 'African philosophy' of which an inherent debate is that of the determination of African identity.

Several efforts have been made by many African scholars on the issue of African predicament adumbrating some factors antecedent to such situation which according to them include slavery and colonialism. Nevertheless, a critical view of the reality of African world leads decisively to a submission that Africa is a problem continent, considering the litany of diseases, famine, wretchedness, corruption that continue to besiege the continent. Consequently, the African predicament is simply pitiable. Sequel to limitations imposed by political and economic constraints. Bakare-Yusuf summarized the African condition as a limit situation. For him, "a limit situation exists where the rules of everyday life have been suspended, and questions of survival are brought to the fore." (www.codesria.org)

In a limit situation, everyday life is laden with uncertainty, tensions, lesion, material scarcity, chaos, genocide, and so no. These and more are factors that constitute the African limit situation in concrete terms. Apart from the afore-mentioned, it is unarguable that the Euro/western view and political representations of Africa contributes considerably to the plight of the content. Africans have been tagged 'irrational' by western scholars. Hegel(1956) consigned Africa to the unhistorical part of the world in his position that:

> What we properly understand by Africa is the unhistorical, undeveloped spirit, still involved in the conditions of mere nature, and which has to be represented here only on the threshold of the world's history.

These debasing notions are still widely propagated all over the west coast irrespective of obvious remedial attempts by African scholars towards reversing the ugly trend. Instead of encouragements, these efforts are met with deliberate resistance such that Bakare comments thus:

> When Africans attempt to refuse this representation and provide a picture of how they make sense of and navigate their world, their words and images are neither heard nor seen. Alternative representations are denied and seen as sheer stupidity, madness and against the rule of rationality. (www.codesria.org)

An unfortunate attendant effect of such circumstance is the tendency of even some African scholars aligning themselves in the trend.

The issue at stake in this discourse is not the denial of the Euro-Western claims as complete fabrications, rather the way in which these negativities are propagated, reflective of politics of representation, whereby difficult life situations are framed in absolute negativity and irredeemable terms. The logical implication of propagated African irrationality remains incivility, incapacity for self-determination, development and self-governance. Hence, African colonization was and is still being projected as a necessity for African remedy without reference to the continent's exploitation by the colonialists. Russell's dehumanizing view of Africans regarding self-governance is quite incisive. He submitted that:

> It would be difficult seriously to advocate the immediate introduction of parliamentary government for the natives of this part of the world, even if it were accompanied by women suffrage and proportional representation. So far as I know, no one supposes the populations of these regions capable of self-determination. (Russell, 1977)

The Euro-Western exploitation of Africa at the wake of colonialism of which representation is usually avoided by the Euro-Western scholars takes a different form in the modern and contemporary era (neo-colonialism and imperialism) in the bid to leave the continent in continuous disintegration and peril. Thus, neo-colonialism remains an indispensable theme in any authentic discourse on the present African predicament. Neo-colonialism represents an avenue for continuous socio-political and economic exploitation and domination of Africa in spite of the continent's acclaimed independence. Its ugly trend is characterized by "expatriate domination of investment opportunities, made possible by access to credit, technology and managerial skills necessary for industrial production." (Akodo & Imbua, 2006)

The neo-colonialist tendencies include a continuous intrusion of the Western world on African economic path, using the continent to achieve developmental goals. Africa thus exploited, continues to wallow in socio-political cum economic poverty as well as developmental sluggishness. The trend is further stretched by culture projection and coercive apparatus through modern technology of which effects remains a cankerworm that feeds deeply into the fabrics of the African cultural value system. In this regaed, Iroegbu(1994) notes that "Western civilization like Western colonization and Christianization came as a superior force, as the true way to success, in fact as the success itself. Africans had simply to adopt them." Hence, the Western imperialist ideal inflicted Africa with its capitalist individualistic model at the expense of the much organic African communalism thereby leaving the continent in utter gullibility and crisis of identity.

So long as globalization is a tool for western holistic integration of varied cultures ensuring social, economic and political dependence, inculcated with the imperialist tendencies, quest for an authentic African advancement remains a toilsome task. A concealed deceptive character of globalization is its tendency of increasing concentration and monopoly of socio-economic resources and power through quest for trans-national co-operations. One of its implications for Africa is that the continent comes under the Euro-Western socio-political and economic control. Khor (2000) refers to the consequence of this situation as "erosion of national sovereignty and narrowed ability of governments and peoples to make choice from options in economic, social and cultural policies." As long as Africans remain under such siege, they remain disoriented, and thus, lack the necessary capabilities for transcending their present situation.

Re-thinking the African Condition: The Levinas' Import

To rethink the African situation is to co-opt agencies (rational) for lifting Africa from its condition. Bakare- Yusuf's attempt at this project is rather interesting. In his "Poetics of the Belly", he adopted Scarry's phenomenology of pain and imagination to drive home his perspective of the African predicament, in the sense that he considered Scarry's universalist phenomenology of pain and imagination as a vital tool for articulation and expression of the historico-existential field of African experience.

According to Scarry, pain admits of no intentional object in the world, rather its object is ontological, that is imagination. In effect, she noted that, "while pain is a state remarkable for being wholly without objects, the imagination is remarkable for being the only state that is wholly its objcts." (Scarry, 1985) While pain is thoroughly of the body, its presence returns the body's experience to that mute and primal moment prior to language, agency, meaning, culture and subjectivity. Hence, structured solely through its objects, the imagination allows for pain to be transposed outside of itself and be projected unto cultural artifacts. In considering the African situation, Bakare submits that "the inseparable conditions of life and structural constraints very often push people to resort to creative means to combat their situation: excessive forms of bodily adornment or expressive trickery and play."(www.codsria.org) Bakare's position is that African situation is that of pain and its attendant imaginative effect produces creativity (work) directed towards alleviation of suffering for the sole purpose of transforming an existential situation. This is equally considered as Bakare's response to the popular Western tag of Africa as more imaginative than rational. Imagination, for him, is an inseparable aspect of African reality, since it remains a relative tool for survival in a critical situation. Bakare considerably collaborates Senghor's widely misunderstood prism, 'Reason is Hellenic and Emotion is African'. Of course, Senghor never ascribed non-rationality to Africa, since reason is the basic defining feature of man. Rather, Senghor would mean that emotion is also an ostensible constituent of man. The West operates more with their head, while Africans dilute the extremities of the head with their hearts.

Bakare's position vehemently challenges the conventional vocabulary of basic need or environmental limitation and places survival on an existential level. It is about how to fuse and satisfy metaphysical, spiritual and existential needs in a way that allows a shout of an emphatic "yes" to the challenges of life. It is about how Africans engage every day in creative practices that tame the horrors of their life, turning their incalculable presence of pain into excessive creativity as evident in cultural artifacts, laughter, drama and the like. This means, as related by Abanuka(1994) that, "if the black people have made no significant breakthrough both in the arts and the sciences, they must still be proud of their distinctive characteristic as a black people."

Being positive about the Africans' imaginative response **to** their existential situation is implied in Levinas' idea in his phenomenology of the 'other'. Levinas' gospel of otherness is informed by a quest for authentic existence and preservation of mankind. It is a call for the reversal of persistent man's inhumanity to man in the face of acclaimed transition from the precarious state of nature to the civil society. The oppressive and exploitative tendencies of man over his fellows are instances of placing the other at the level of mere phenomenal objects, as tools for personal gratification. In such instance, self interest is placed as premium at the wake of interaction while the good of the other is utterly neglected and relegated.

In the case of Africa, her colonialists and slave traders were not primarily concerned about the continent's civilization and development. Whatever civilization presently evident in Africa would only be providential when considered vis-à-vis the plunder and exploitation of the continent by the colonialists. It is simply a case of Levinas' idea of looking at the other as a mere object of the self. The consequence of colonialism on African remains unarguably obvious. The denial of African rationality and possible civility is borne out of epistemological bias which only seeks self satisfaction at the expense of true knowledge, which Levinas considers a misplacement of philosophical priority.

If ontology does not accord adequate importance to the good of the other, ethics should be first philosophy since in ethics, the otherness of the other is given a veritable consideration. Levinas advocacy is in line with Augustine's view on the ethics of love and care for one another which eschews ego-centricism. Thus Augustine in Mellway(2009) states that:

> A love that rejoices in a good that is at once shared by all and unchanging- a love that makes 'one heart' out of many, a love that is the whole hearted and harmonious obedience of mutual affection.

Despite the plundering of Africa in the colonial period, the continent continues to suffer ideological, social, economic and political violence, such that the greatest challenge of African diaspora is racism. In his philosophy of otherness, Levinas desires is to make postulations for the thriving of human freedom, the denial of which is evident in racism, colonialism, slavery, imperialism and neo-colonialism. For instance, Levinas' postulation would condemn the European colonial philosophy which "preached an epistemology that views the African incapable of scientific or philosophical destiny, potentiality and practice." (Osuagwu, 1999) The persistent biased Western ideological representations of Africa, since the image of African world currently in circulation is a literal incarnation of a negative dialectic, amount to a refusal to uphold the otherness of African essence.

The remedial import of Levinas' otherness on African condition remains the need to look at Africa objectively with a view to lifting it from its present predicament and placing it on the appropriate developmental pedestal. It entails African freedom from all forms of neo-colonial exploitations and imperialism. Levinas advocacy is in line with David Hume's moral theory. According to Hume, "we are rationally committed to acting justly by our very practices designed to promote common or complimentary interests." (The Encyclopedia Of Philosophy,1967) It must be noted that Levinas' project does not deny the importance of inter-subjectivity. Rather, it posits that the good of the other should be accorded a fair consideration for the sole purpose of the good of mankind in general. Hence in the African situation, Levinas would call for an adequate none exploitation but a regenerative inter-continental relation which equally places importance on African development, since the face-to face relation presupposes an unlimited and committed obligation to the other.

Equally, Levinas' prayer would be to uphold and appreciate the African nature and adaptation to her existential situations. It demands respect for the *Africanity* of the African of which Nnabugwu(2005) opines that "as human beings, we are all separate individuals but with a common destiny." This entails, in line with Bakare's ideal, a clarion call for the acceptance of African modes of investment in corporeal practices and cultural performance in the midst of existential chaos as a "will to power" that transcends the conventional vocabulary of crises articulated solely in terms of a purely physical need or environmental limitation.

Conclusion

A view of Africa from the developmental perspective relegates the continent to a problematic plane. Although several efforts have been made to compel an adequate understanding and articulation of the factors responsible for African predicament, it must be agreed that irrespective of the civilization brought to African through colonialism, the ugly aspect of the trend leaves nothing much to be desired.

As already shown within the course of this paper, Levinas' concept of Otherness has a pivotal role to play towards African redemption. It is therefore strongly suggested that its prospects be adequately relayed and utilized as a sure justification of Levinas' sincere and laudable intellectual effort as well as an indication that the world societies have transcended rational biases to pave way for the appreciation of objective intellectual endeavours.

References

Abanuka, B (1994), *A New Essay on African Philosophy*, Enugu : Snaap Press Ltd.,7.

Akodo, W. & Imbua, D (2006), "Waving Through History: Nigeria in the International Community and the Challenge of Development" in **Unizik Journal of Arts and Humanities** vol. 8, September, 89.

Hegel, G.W.F(1956), *The Philosophy of History*, New York: Dover Publications Inc., 99.

http://www.codsria.org/Archives/galO/papers_ga10_12/Economics_Yusuf.htm

http:/www..wikipaedia.com/other_Levinas_Emmanuel/pg_20_htm.asp

Iroegbu, P (1994), *Enwisdomization and African Philosophy*,Owerri: International Universities Press Ltd., 80.

Khor, M (2000), *Globalization and the South: Some Critical Issues*, Abuja : Spectrum, 4.

Mellway,J., on http://enlightenment.supersaturated.com/essays/test/jamiemellway/Augustine.html

Nnabugwu, M.B (2005), *Africa in the March of Civilization*, Enugu : Quintagon Publishers, 167- 68.

Osuagwu, I.M (1999), *A Contemporary History of African Philosophy*, Enugu: Snaap Press Ltd,176.

Routledge Encyclopedia of Philosophy,(1998) London : Routledge, 580.

Russell, B (1977), *Roads to Freedom*, London: Unwin Paperbacks, 121.

Scarry, E (1985), *The Body in Pain:The Making and Unmaking of the World*, New York & London : Oxford University Press, 162.

The Encyclopedia of Philosophy, (1967)Vol. 3 & 4, London: Collier Macmillan Publishers, 299

CHAPTER THREE

IMMORTALITY IN TIV THOUGHT

Paul T. Haaga, Ph.D & Aye, Aondongu Joseph

Executive Summary

Immortality in Tiv Thought: A Philosophical Appraisal" is an inquiry into the Tiv concept of immortality. The question of immortality is no doubt a crucial issue that stems from the inner recesses of man in his attempt to define his destiny. The Tiv from whose perspective this paper is anchored are also deeply concerned about this issue and seek to address it in the best way possible. The thrust of this paper is an attempt to philosophically appraise the concept of immortality from the perspective of the Tiv of central Nigeria. This paper seeks to venture the Tiv conception of immortality which has received little attention from scholars especially that of Tiv extraction. In its inquiry the paper adapts an interpretative approach to arrive at its findings. From its investigation, the paper posits that the Tiv explicitly express belief in immortality though from an anthropomorphic standpoint. The paper seeks to contribute to the corpus of knowledge in the subject matter from the perspective understudy.

Keyword: Immortality, Soul, Conception, Tiv, *Uma*

Introduction

It is quite apparent that what makes a man to be a man is not to have a body or life or emotions (animals have all these too) but to have rationality and intellect, powers which are spiritual. This implies that the "substantial form" of man or what makes a man to be a man must be a "formal act" or principle of life (Soul) whose nature is spiritual and which actualizes the body and its potencies. This spirituality of the human soul makes it a very special type of substantial form, since it has "subsistence" of its own. This implies that the human soul is immortal.

Much has been said and written on the subject of immortality of the soul from antiquity to the present, scholars of various disciplines have expounded on the subject from philosophers, theologians, religionists, psychologists, poets and even scientists. However, the mystery surrounding this issue is yet to unravel. While some express belief in it, some see it as a mere human fantasy. The veil demarcating the spatio-temporal world and the world that lies beyond is yet to be clearly lifted. How can an immaterial soul and the body which is material coexist to form a substantial unity? Such questions have been asked and answered variously in form of proofs.

The question of the soul and immortality transcends scholarship; it is a question that emanates from the inner recesses of man. As a question involving the collective destiny of man as a whole, it ought to be considered from the perspective of the individual and collective experience of man in his various cultures and belief systems.

Blaise Paschal in (Guersart 1975:14) observes that, what is at stake here is not for rational consideration alone. Rational knowledge satisfies the intellect not the emotions and appetite. The implication of this is that the question of immortality is at the core of man's existence.

In most African cultures, man belongs to two worlds; the material and the world of the hereafter. There is however an ontological relation between all reality as a whole. The world is seen as living, active and dynamic unity in which material and spiritual beings find their place (Nwigwe 2001:3) the concept immortality features prominently in the African spirit world. The African concept of Immortality is anthropocentric. For the Traditional African, one enters into personal immortality at death when there are people to remember him especially his or her children. however he enters into collective immortality when all who knew him have died. He becomes a member of the family of spirits who are believed to occupy the ontological state between God and men. (Uduigwomen 1995:80) Death therefore is the beginning of a permanent ontological departure of the individual from mankind to spirithood. The Tiv from whose perspective this study is premised shares to some extent in the foregoing.

TivPhilosophico – Religious World View

The Tiv are presently found in Benue State in North Central Nigeria. Social research about the Tiv ethnic group spanned many years. There are various versions concerning the origin of the Tiv people. Various scholars both early and modern have contradicted themselves about Tiv origin, (Gbenda 2005:71) One school of thought traced Tiv origin to a certain "Shon" who was said to have two sons "Oryian" and "Orii". Oryian Means white man while "Orii" means black man from whom Tiv descended (Moti and Wegh 2001:9).Another version traced Tiv ancestor to one "Takuruku" who had two sons; Tiv and Uke; Uke refers to all non Tiv. The reference to "Takuruku" is however contentious as many Tiv did not conceive of him as a human being but some kind of music to announce the death of someone (Moti and Wegh 2001:10) Tiv had two sons i.e "Ichongo" and "Ipusu". The Tiv are descended from Tiv two sons" Ichongo" and "Ipusu". This segmentation is reflected in Tiv Socio-Political Organization.

According to some versions, the Tiv are said to have originated and migrated from the Bantu of Southern Africa, though the Congo Region of Central Africa, across the mountains of Cameroon to the Benue valley in the 16th and 17th centuries (Makar 1975:28).Religion is no doubt a most embracing subject. Tiv philosophy and religion is subsumed under this assertion. Tiv religion seems ambiguous and often times bizarre because of the complex nature of the subject matter. Religion in Tiv worldview does not present a consistent picture to elicit a clear understanding. Tiv religion and philosophy can only be understood when viewed from a holistic perspective, where man, nature and the supernatural constitute a continuum (Moti and Wegh 2001:19).

Tiv: Philosophico – religious worldview like most Africans acknowledges the existence of a supernatural being called "Aondo" (God). Aondo is the creator of the universe and everything in it including man, man is the crown of creation. There is also a strong belief in "Akombo" (Cosmo – Supernatural forces). Through the instrumentality of Akombo, man participates in the creative work of Aondo (God) by ensuring the ordering of society. Akombo is synonymous with Tiv religion since you cannot talk of Tiv religion in Isolation of Akombo. Akombo are represented in cultic emblems and touches almost all aspects of Tiv life. Abraham (33:62) attests to this by identifying eight areas in which Akombo are employed: illness, birth, fertility of crops, rendering arrows efficacious, hunting, good luck, obtaining wives etc.Another fundamental element of Tiv religion is "Tsav" (witchcraft). For the Tiv, Tsav is a mystical power, it is a tangible and intangible mysterious power. Tsav is normally neutral deployed for both good and evil proposes depending on the disposition of the carrier Bohannan (1965:513), Downes (1971:18), Moti and Wegh (2001:58) hold that, Tsav is related to life itself and it is used as a means of social control to maintain law and order, it occupies a prominent place in Tiv social organization both ideological and functionally.

The Concept of Immortality: Philosophical Perspective

Immortality generally implies the continuity of human spiritual existence after the death of the body. This is both a philosophical and religious view. It is pertinent to note that this concept is distinct from bodily resurrection. Apart from Pythagoras who also has influence on Plato, Plato (428 – 348 B.C) was the first thinker from the west to systematically address the issue of immortality, it was one of the main problems of his thought. With the contention that reality as such is fundamentally spiritual, Plato tried to prove immortality maintaining that nothing could destroy the soul. According to Plato, the soul is self- moving, un-generated and eternal. The soul according to him came into the world from the world of forms after its liberation. (Encyclopedia Britannica Vol. 26).

Albertus Magnus (Encyclopedia Britannica Vol. 26) defined immortality on the basis that the soul in itself is a cause, an independent reality. This assertion by Magnus implies that the soul is ungenerated andsimple, hence it is not subject to the body. Benedict Spinoza (1652 – 1677) saw God as ultimate reality, hence he maintains his eternity but not the immortality of individual persons within him. According to him all things are only the modifications of God who is the ultimate and eternal reality. The German philosopher Gottfried Wilhelm Leibniz (1666 – 1716) contended that, reality is constituted of spiritual monads. Human beings as finite monads not capable of origination by composition are created by God, he could also annihilate them.

However, in that he has planted in men a striving for spiritual perfection, there may be faith that he will ensure their continual existence, thus giving them the possibility to achieve this.

George Hegel's (1770 – 1931) idea of immortality is subsumed in his idea of the absolute. For him, God is the absolute and everything is a manifestation of that absolute including the soul which will also go back to the absolute. Emmanuel Kant (1724 – 1841) contended that immortality of the soul is an essential requirement of morality. Man should conform to the moral law through the practice of virtue. However, in no instance of his existence is a rational being capable of realizing perfect virtue. Therefore Kant concluded that this perfection can be attained through an indefinite progress and indefinite existence. This indefinite progress is only possible in an indefinite duration of the existence of this same rational being which is called immortality.

Rene Descartes concept of man implies immortality because he conceives man as mind (Soul) that happens to have a body, but which is not an essential part of its nature. St Augustine of Hippo (354 – 430) conception of man is that of a "rational soul using a body". Thus as a Platonist, Augustine argues that the Soul obtains truth in intellective knowledge. He remarked that the soul is immaterial and is superior to the body, therefore, it cannot be acted upon by the body, hence it is immortal (Frost 62:32).

Thomas Aquinas though and Aristotelian parted ways with his tradition concerning the issue of immortality of the soul and clinged to the Platonic tradition. He argued that the Soul is not intrinsically dependent on the body, for it cannot be affected by the death and corruption of the body. He maintained that the soul is immaterial otherwise it would be incapable of reflecting on itself or apprehending abstract knowledge. St Thomas further stressed that, the Soul naturally desire immortality, since this desire is natural, then it cannot be in vain (Summa theological 19,75).

St Bonaventure (1221 – 274) conceives the soul as composed of form and spiritual substance which he calls "spiritual matter". As such, the soul is not intrinsically dependent on the body, it can be separated from the body and exist without the body. He uses both Augustinian and Aristotelian arguments to prove the immortality of the soul. First, that the human soul derives perfect happiness, secondly he based his argument on the necessity for adequate sanction for the violation or observance of the natural law. He based another argument on the independence of intellectual activities of the body. The soul's natural faculty carries out reflective activities without expending physical energy that shows its superiority. Finally he held that the fact that the soul is capable of grasping the eternal truths shows that it is of the same nature as these truths namely, immaterial, immutable, eternal and indestructible.

African Concept of Immortality

In almost all African cultures there is a belief in the afterlife, however, with varying degrees. According to Mbiti (1969:27) death is a process which removes a person gradually from the living to the living dead. After death, the individual is believed to continue existing in the world and is remembered by relative and friends who know him in this life and who have survived him.

This is referred to as living dead and this is also a state of personal immortality. With time however, such a person sinks beyond personal immortality to collective immortality which is the state of the spirit. The belief in the continuation of life in the spirit world leads to burial rites to ensure a place in the invisible world, (Ela 93:14). Dopamu (79:253) Opined that the washing of the corpse and burying a person with material things as is the case in some African cultures signifies getting ready for the journey to the next world. Commenting on the Igbo culture, Nwigwe (2001:23) observes that, death does not involve the separation of body and soul and that it is not explicit what happens at death. The Igbo rather see death as a change from one state of existence to another (Kanu 2015:228).

In consonance with the foregoing, Nabofa in Adegbola (1983:17) maintains that, there is a general consensus in Urhobo thought that after death, the soul (Erhi) passes into another world which is known as "Erivbin". However, there are also others who hold that the dead only change their places of abode on this earth. This implies that such people only go to live in other places other than theirs and continue with their normal lives. This belief is flawed in the sense that, the glimpse of a stranger remotely resembling the dead person from a particular place is no proof enough to conclude that such a deceased person is actually residing in another place on earth with all his physical and daily attributes. These views among other invariably affirm immortality and that the living dead are always around.

Opoku (1978:21) is of the view that the dead only go on a journey and that death does not end life. The present life is seen as a preparation for the journey into after life where the dead continue to live. Even in the afterlife Opoku contends that the dead are not cut off from the living as they continue to reveal themselves in dreams or appear to their living relatives. Africans see immortality as consisting in the act of procreation. This explains the significant role of marriage in African societies, unless a person has children to remember him and carry his name after his death, he is soon forgotten and sinks into oblivion. It is incumbent upon every mature African to get married with the intent of having children especially males in order not to be cut off from immortality.

The general African approach to the question of immortality is anthropocentric rather than spiritual. This is because the Africans see life beyond the grave as neither better nor worse than life on earth because they have no way of knowing so they consider if unattractive. This explains why emphasis is placed on life in the world than beyond; and this consists in the accumulation of as many children as possible. This ensures interminable life here on earth.

Tiv Concept of the Nature of the Soul

Part of the problem of western teaching on the soul is that of definition. Every reality is defined by making it fit into the scheme of definition through genus and specific difference.

The African belief system is both less and more than philosophy. In African thought there is an ontological relation between all things, however, the material things serve merely as vessels through which spiritual forces manifest themselves, such entities are believed to have existence of their own. In most African cultures there is no sharp dualism in the relationship between body and soul. This is because death is not conceived as a separation of body and soul, but rather a change from one state of existence to another. The body is applied not just to stand for the physical body but the totality of man because the bodily organs are believed to exercise mental functions.

The Tiv world is a psyco-spiritual one in which everything visible has its equivalent in the invisible sphere of life. Man is conceived as a composite of material and spiritual elements. The material aspect is "Iyol" (body) while the spiritual is "Jijingi" (Spirit). This "Jijingi" is the life force of man, it is demonstrated by the shadow cast by the body. Spirit and soul are used interchangeably since there is no sharp distinction between the two in Tiv thought. The soul is seen as imperishable while the body is perishable. The Tiv believe that at death, the spirit (Jijingi) leaves the body, it doesn't die with the body. It is believed that it hovers around the dead body before departing. This "Jijingi" is not just a shadow, but a reflection of life (Uma) which is also construed as the soul in man. (Gbenda 2005:17) the soul or "Jijingi" (Spirit) is believed to have endless life since it has a divine origin and therefore indestructible. (Hulugh 2014).

Immortality in Tiv thought

In Tiv society according to Gbenda (2005), marriage brings out clearly eschatological ideals of eternal life. This is because children are a product of marriage and the main purpose of marriage is for continuity in the transmission of life. An unmarried man in Tiv traditional thought is to some extent considered irresponsible hence he cannot be trusted with responsibility. Tarbo (1980:56) Opine thus, "to the Tiv, having children means eternal life.It means to cooperate with God for the continuityof one's life and the community in general.

Parents look forward to seeing their grand children before they die". This assures them of the continuation of their generation. A man who among other things has married many wives and has many children is said to be "Shagbaor" (Greatman), at his death he is said not to have died but to have "oughaough" (Sloughed off) and continue living in his children. The values and ideals of the family are also expected to be immortalized in the children.

Like the sophists, the Tiv regard man as the measure of all things and the world and life are centredaround man, therefore in every facet of life, the Tiv hold that man must be preeminent. Questions of immortality and afterlife are approached from an anthropocentric dimension. Procreative activity is taken seriously in Tivsociety, issues of child care are accorded proper attention.It is pertinent to note that most "Akombo" (Cosmo-supernatural forces) are in one way or the other concerned with the well being and survival of the family.

In Tiv tradition, a new born child of all polluting influences (Moti and Wegh 2001:23). "Tyumbun" and "iee" enhances the child's health and growth. All this is geared towards sustaining and perpetuating one's lineage.

Conclusion

Man has always been an enigma to himself. He has sought answers to questions such as who is man? What constitute man? What is his purpose and mission in the world? These questions have always perplexed and intrigued man. To these questions various answers and solutions have been proffered by scholars of various disciplines and schools. In view of the foregoing, man has refused to see life as factitious but has tried to find meaning in life. The concept of immortality will continue to be relevant as long as man lives in the world. Because it is at the core of human existence, it is an issue that is fundamental to human life and our attitudes to it determines our entire attitude to life itself. This piece in conclusion established that the Tivlike other Africans believe in immortality though with their own peculiarities. For the Tiv, the spirit or soul of man does not cease to exist with the death of the body. The soul continue to live and there is a strong belief that the souls of the living dead gather to rest after their sojourn on earth at a blissful place. Also, the Tivconception of immortality is anthropocentric and consists in having as many children as possible to perpetuate one's lineage. They also express immortality in names. Names such as "Orbeenga" (Man never cease to exist) are suggestive of immortality and express the Tiv belief that man will never cease to exist even in death, he lives on in his children.

References

Abraham, R.C. "The Tiv people" Lagos: Government Printer 193.

Abraham, R.C. "The Tiv Religion" London: Crown Agency 1940.

Aquinas, T. "Summa Theological 1, 75,2.

Bohannan, A. "Who are the Tiv?: A Socio-Culture Inquiry into TivQynamics" in P.T. Ahire (ed) The Tiv in Contemporary, Nigeria, Zaria Writers Organization 1993.

Downes, R.M. "Tiv Religion" Ibadan: University Press, 1971.

Dupamu, P.A. &Awolalu, J.O. "West African Religion" Ibadan: Onibonoje Press (Nig) Ltd, 1970.

Ela, J.M. "My Faith as an African" London: Geoffrey Chapman, 1993.

Frost, S. "Basic Teaching of the great philosophers" New York: Doubleday Publishing Group Inc, 1962.

Gbenda, J.S. "Eschatology in Tiv Traditional Religious Culture: An Interpretative Enquiry" Nsukka: Chuka Educational Publishers, 2005.

Gilson, E. "History of Christian Philosophy in the middle ages" London: Methuen, 1955.

Guersart, M. (ed) "Les Penses de B. Paschal" Paris: Gonsel, 1975.

Kanu, I. A. (2015). *A hermeneutic approach to African Traditional Religion*. Nigeria: Augustinian Publications.

Metuh, E.I "African Religion in Western conceptual Schemes" Jos: Imico Press, 1985.

Moti, J.S. &Wegh, F.S. "An Encounter BetweenTiv Religion and Christianity" Enugu: Snaap Press. 2001.

Nabofa, N.Y. "Erhi and Eschatogy" in Adegbola (ed) Traditional; Religion in West Africa. Ibadan: Selfer Books Ltd, 1983.

Nwigwe, B.E. "the concept of immortality of the soul in classical Western Philosophy and Igbo Culture: An essay in conceptual Analysis" West African Journal of Philosophy. Vol 4. 2001.

Omoregbe J. "A simplified history of Western Philosophy" Vol. 11, Lagos: Joja Educational Publishers Ltd., 1991.

Opoku, K.A. "West African Traditional Religion" Accra: Fep International Publishing Ltd, 1978.

Tarbo, N.N "Marriage among the Tiv" Rome: Pontifical Urbaniana University, 1980.

Uduigwomen, A.F (ed) "Footmarks on African Philosophy" Lagos: Obaroh and Ogbinaka publishers Ltd, 1995.

CHAPTER FOUR

AFRICAN ENVIRONMENTAL ETHICS: A NON –ANTHROPOCENTRIC AFRICAN ENVIRONMENTALISM

Chinedu Stephen Ifeakor & Andrew Otteh

Executive Summary

Africa today is faced with several environmental issues ranging from gully erosions, desertification, flooding, overpopulation, water pollution and Co2 emissions from cars and engines et cetera. Two factors responsible for these are: the aging earth and the activities of humans. Environmental ethics therefore seeks for the extension of moral community to include the ecosystem as a whole. African environmental ethics therefore is an enquiry into the thought system and ontology of the Africans on the environment. This paper looks at the theories and conceptions put forward by scholars in their bid to evolving a promising non anthropocentric African environmentalism. Oruka and Jumia's Parent earth ethics, Ogungbemi's ethics of nature relatedness, Tangwa's eco-bio-communitarianism, Mogobe Ramose's Ubuntu ecology, Behren's African relational environmentalism et cetera. In the journey so far, using the philosophical method of analyses, one observes that these theories are either not African at all, judging from African ontological system or not African enough in the sense of not reflecting one important aspect of African ontology.I propose however, that obligatory anthropoholism is a more promising African environmental attitude. My view gives a sense in which humans have a pride of place in African ontology (obligation). It also stresses the developmental implications for the African continent.

Introduction

Challenges to our environment in the 21st century have been an issue of great concern. Few factors in the writer's view have contributed to these challenges. The first is nature. By this I mean ageing world and its implications. This means that an old man cannot but be old in the bones with shrinked body no matter how much health care and food that is given to him/her. The world is not getting any younger and so we see some of its implications on the environment. The second factor and the most important one too, is the activities of man. Science and technology brought with it industrialization. Even though man has tried to explore and improve her life on earth, it came with some disadvantages. In environmental ethics, there is this presumption that if the activities of human kind can be directed aright, the environment can be saved from further degradation. Thus environmental ethics is an attempt to prescribe to humankind the right way to relate to the environment so as to preserve our environment. While ethics deals with rights and wrongs, good and bad in the realms of human conduct, environment ethics deals with rights and wrongs, good and bad in our relationship to the environment.

The need for reorientation is now as 21st century is experiencing serious environmental degradation. Let us see some of these challenges; Pollution: Pollution of air, water and soil require millions of years to recoup. Industry and motor vehicles exhaust are the number one pollutants, heavy metals, nitrates and plastic are toxins responsible for pollution while water pollution is caused by oil spill, acid rain, urban runoff, air pollution is caused by various gasses and toxins released by industries and factories and combustion of fossil fuels, soil pollution is majorly caused by industrial waste that deprives soil from essential nutrients. Climatic changes like global warming is the result of human practices like emission of Greenhouse gasses. Global warming leads to rising tempretures of the oceans and the earth surface, melting of pollar ice caps, rise in sea levels and also unnatural patterns of precipitation such as flash floods, excessive snow or dissertification. Overpopulation: The population of the planet is reaching unsustainable levels as it faces shortages of resources like water, fuel and food. Population explosion in less developed and developing countries are straining the already scarce resources. Intensive agriculture practiced to produce food damage the environment through use of chemical fertilizers, pesticides and insecticides. Overpopulation is one of the crucial current environmental problems. Natural Resources Depletion: Fossil fuel consumption results in emission of Greenhouse gasses, which is responsible for global warming and climate change. Globally, people are taking efforts to shift to renewable sources of energy like solar, wind, biogas and geothermal energy.

The cost of installing the infrastructure and maintaining these sources has pummeled in the recent years. Waste Disposal: The over consumption of resources and creation of plastics are creating a global crisis of waste disposal. Developed countries are notorious for producing an excessive amount of waste or garbage and dumping their waste in the oceans and, less developed countries. Nuclear waste disposal has tremendous health hazards associated with it. Plastic, fast food, packaging and cheap electronic waste threaten the well being of humans.

Climate change: Climate change is yet another environmental problem that has surfaced in the last couple of decades. It occurs due to rise in global warming which occurs due to increase in temperature of atmosphere by burning of fossil fuels and release of harmful gasses by industries. Climate change has various harmful effects but not limited to melting polar ice, change in seasons, and occurrence of new diseases. Frequent occurrence of floods and change in overall weather scenario. Loss of biodivisersity: Human activity is leading to the extinction of species and habitats and loss of bio-diversity. Ecosystem, which took millions of years to perfect, are in danger when any species population is decimating. Balance of natural processes like pollination is crucial to the survival of the eco-system and human activity threatens the same. Another example is the destruction of coral reefs in the various oceans, which support the rich marine life. Deforestation: Our forests are natural sinks of carbon dioxide and produce fresh oxygen as well as helps in regulating temperature and rainfall. At present forests cover 30% of the land but every year tree cover is lost due to growing population and its growing demand for more food, shelter and clothing. Deforestation simply means cleaning of green cover making such land available for residential, industries and commercial purpose. Ocean Acidification: It is a direct impact of excessive production of Co_2. The ocean acidity has increased by the last 250 years but by 2100, it may shoot up by 150%.

This has great impact on shellfish, Plankton as well as humans. Ozone layer Depletion: The ozone layer is an invisible layer of protection around the planet that protects us from the sun's harmful rays. This depletion is as a result of pollution caused by chlorine and bromide found in chloro-floro Carbon (CFCs). Once these toxic gasses reach the upper atmosphere, they cause a hole in the ozone layer, the biggest of which is above the Antarctic. Ozone layer is valuable because it prevents harmful ultra violet radiation from reaching the earth. This is one of the most important current environmental problems.

Acid Rain: Acid rain occurs due to the presence of certain pollutants in the atmosphere. Acid rain can be caused due to combustion of fossil fuels or erupting volcanoes or rotting vegetation which release Sulfur dioxide and nitrogen into the atmosphere. Acid rain is a known environmental problem that can have serious effect on human health, wildlife and aquatic species. Genetic Engineering: Genetic modification of food using biotechnology is called genetic engineering. Genetic modification of food results in increased toxins and diseases as genes from an allergic plant can transfer to target plant. Genetically modified crops can cause serious environmental problems as an engineered gene may prove toxic to wildlife.[1] Humans have greatly contributed to these environmental problems as it is the activities going on in factories, industries, urban areas, etc. that cause these problems.

Human technology in general, and biotechnology (agricultural and human) in particular, have narrowed the gap between the natural and the artificial between nature and humanity, between "God's work" and "work of human hands" to the extent that some have proclaimed God and/or nature dead. Human tinkering with nature, which can be said to have begun with the discovery of agriculture about ten millennia ago, and which seems both inescapable and unobjectionable, has evolved, (thanks to modern technology) into wholesome interventions in the process of nature, exemplified by the engineering of novel artificial life forms. Such developments have gradually turned the perennial moral concern with the physical environment and with medical practice info moral disquiet and even moral alarm.

As Frederick Ferre pointedly remarked at the Nairobi World Conference of Philosophy on Philosophy, Humanity and the Environment;

> By the time organisms are sufficiently artificial to be patentable, it is clear that the relative weights of nature and culture have reversed themselves. Culture is in the driver's seat and nature is hanging on for dear life (literally) as we hurtle down unexplored roads with poor visibility, and with uninspected and untried brakes.[2]

The cogency of this remark made before mammalian cloning became a scientific fact in 1997, is today even more evident than before. Nevertheless, biotechnology also holds a certain justified fascination for human beings, because of its positive potential in such domains as preventive and therapeutic medicine and in agriculture.

In the face of these developments, human ethical sensibilities and responsibilities are urgently called for. As human beings, we carry the whole weight of moral responsibility and obligation for the world on our shoulders. The claim that human kind is the apex of biological existence as we know it; has sometimes been dismissed as an arrogant spiciest claim and contested by some human militants for the rights of animals and/or plants less disputable however, is the fact that while human beings have putative moral responsibilities toward inanimate objects, plants and the animals, these later cannot be considered, without absurdity, as having any reciprocal moral obligation toward humans. Human intervention in nature could plausibly be justified by appeal to this asymmetrical responsibility, although this does not imply that every intervention is justifiable. For these reasons, our focus on eco-ethics, environmental ethics, developmental ethics, medical ethics, bioethics – all of which can be gathered into one basket labeled "eco-bioethics" is not only appropriate but also quite timely.[3]

In African background this search for harmony is important for few reasons; African perspective is important because the world is searching for theories which will help man conserve the environment, Africa being a part of this whole can contribute through their thought towards this project. Secondly, if the world will come to value their environment, they have to be conscientized and taught to, Eugene Hargrove commented that teachers of environmental philosophy in developing or evolving theories that will enable them teach their students, should be careful not to import from other cultures but to look into the ontology of such people there will be rich cultural or ontological materials which will enhance effective communication of values for the conservation of the environment. Thirdly, Huttington's clash of civilization teaches the world that every culture or civilization brings something important to the world table Africa being rich in culture and civilization can lend voice to the search for ethical attitude of mankind to the environment.

It have been held by scholars like J, Baird Callicott, J.S. Mbiti, Benezeth Bujo et cetera that African ontology is anthropocentric, however, African scholars as Ogungbemi, Behrens, Chemhuru, Ekwealor have argued and strongly too that African ontology and environmental understanding is non anthropocentric. Time may not allow for detailed analyses of these arguments both for and against anthropocentrism, we simply seek to look at the theories so far put forward by some African environmental ethicists in their effort to evolving a promising non anthropocentric African environmental ethics.

For a theory to be fully African, it has to show mastery of African ontology otherwise it lacks the characteristics of being African. The human being and the interconnectedness of being are two of the salient values in African ontology which are relevant to the environment. These two values have been erroneously interpreted in various ways. For instance, the pride of place of the human being in African ontology has been described as anthropocentric by Kai Horthenske, Ramose in his Ecology through Ubuntu posited that humans in African ontology are part of the whole of ecosystem but "a privileged part", Thad Metz in his relational theory of moral status posited that it is the relationship "with human" that confers moral status to other beings in the ecosystem. I argue in this paper that while Horthenske's anthropocentric stance on Africa is untenable, Ramose failed to give the sense in which the human being is a privileged part of the ecosystem. Also Thad Metz failed to give us the sense in which it is the relationship with humans in particular that confers moral status. It is human capacity for obligation, for action, for taking responsibility that singles her out in the ecosystem. The privilege humans enjoy stems from the fact that he is saddled with the responsibility of tending, caring for the whole of the ecosystem which he is a part. I call it obligatory anthropoholism. This paper is divided into four parts; the introduction, African environmental theories so far, obligatory anthropoholism as a viable African environmental ethics and conclusion.

Theories in African Environmental Ethics: An Attempt at Evolving a Promising African Non anthropocentric Environmental Ethics

A look at some theories put forward by African environmental ethicists in their attempt at evolving a non anthropocentric African environmental ethics is necessary for some reasons. Firstly, examining what have been done so far enables the researcher to stand on the shoulder of scholars to see clearer, valuing the contributions of scholars makes for academic humility since it simply imply that just as the weaknesses of their theories are shown here, so also will the weakness of my own attempt be shown by others. Secondly, in the works of other theorists, one discovers a lacuna that forms the real reason for writing. In the theories we will be looking at, careful scrutiny will show that the place of man is conspicuously missing and where it is shown, as in Ubuntu Ecology and Relational environmentalism, they failed to give the sense in which humans are a privileged part of the whole ecosystem. The failure to give this sense reduces their work somewhat to anthropocentrism. However, we are simply doing an attempt, not claiming mastery, nor saying that ours is all there is and should be in African environmental ethics. Ours is also a contribution to scholarship and an attempt at given perspective to African environmental philosophy.

We will look at Ogungbemi's ethics of nature relatedness, Tangwa's eco-bio-communitariam, Odera Oruka and Jumia's Parental earth ethics. We will also explore the strengths and weaknesses of Ramose's Ecology through Ubuntu and finally Kelvin Behrens' African Relational environmentalism. Let us start with Ogungbemi's ethics of nature relatedness.

2.1. Ethics of Nature –Relatedness

Segun Ogungbemi in his paper *"An African perspective in the environmental crisis"*[1] discusses the nature of the environmental crisis in Africa. In doing this, he came to a number of conclusions concerning the principle causes of the environmental crisis in African and proposes some ethical reflection and practical suggestions on how to mitigate the challenge posed by the environmental crisis

Ogungbemi construes environmental crisis in global content and as one of the greatest global problem of our time. In his thinking, environmental crisis is a conjunction of some natural disaster such as earthquake, volcanic eruption and storms together with man's activity of exploration and utilization of natural resources such as through the ingenuity of science and technology, which have impacted negatively on the environment and human well being. While recognizing the universality of the environmental crisis, Ogungbem notes that in understanding the nature of environmental crisis within the context of sub-Saharan Africa, three points are sacrament. First, ignorance and poverty. Secondly, science and technology and thirdly, political conflict, including international economic pressures.[4] He argues that in order to properly understand the nature of the environmental crisis in Africa, we need to understand the ways in which both traditional and modern social structure have led to environmental degradation.

On the factor of ignorance and poverty, Ogungbem explains that the majority of traditional Africans live in rural areas where the people wallow in poverty and lack of basic amenities such as good water supplies, adequate lavatories and proper energy use. As a consequence, the rivers were polluted with human waste exposing the people to avoidable water borne diseases such as dysentery, typhoid and cholera. The excessive use of fuel wood and constant bush burning which is a predominant practice in traditional Africa, increases air pollution, affects air quality and depletes the forest and other natural habitats. This factor of poverty cum ignorance on the part of traditional Africans Ogungbemi argues, does not necessarily exonerate our people from their contribution to environmental hazard.[3] This is particularly so given that the relevant patterns of behaviour may come at least in part from an inability to exploit nature because of low levels of economic and technological development.

Besides the crude contribution of traditional African societies to the world environmental crisis mention most be mode of the more catastrophic contribution of modern African to the environmental crisis, Ogungbemi recognizes the drive to catch up with the developmental pace of the western world by African states government as responsible for the mass destruction of our ecosystem through unguided explorative engagements with African natural resources, the flora and Fauna. Many African nations are resource rich, but because their economies are not structured to take full advantage of these resources, they are exported with little or no value added. The net results are relativity few jobs and other economic advantages (and what advantages there are often siphoned off by the corrupt elite) and considerable environmental damage. Moreover, the damage often results in loss of agricultural land that the poor rely upon, and significant pollution of waterways.

Water is another essential natural resource that has been adversely affected in modern African through human activities. the deposition and dumping of toxic waste on the African coasts and inland by industries both within and outside the continent, pollute the water through oil exploration and defacto spillage, and through bacteriological and chemical agents like fertilizers have made our waters unsafe not only for humans but also for other species in our waters.

Ogumbegmi further pointed out how air which is an essential natural resource for living has been threatened by human techno- scientific activities. Most fundamental in this regard is the uncontrolled nature of the emissions coming out from automobile industrial machine, artillery air raids and such like. In addition to the causes of pollution of air, land and water in Africa, Ogumgbemi equally identified the unprecedented population growth in contemporary African as another factor that has continued to aggravate the destruction of the environment in Africa. The logic here of simple; the more the population, the more the stress on the natural resources and consumption ipso factor increase. More consumption results in more disposal of waste and where waste is carelessly managed as it is the case in many African states, the more hazardous the environment is prone to. It needs be stated however, that Ogumbemi posited that it is not clear that population by itself is the key problem rather it is inequitable distribution of global on earth.[6]

Granted that many African traditional folks as well as their contemporary counterparts have in some ways contributed to the general environment problems of the world today, Ogmgbemi equally underscores how traditional Africa has lived with nature with respect and awe. He writes in traditional environmental management thus;

> In our traditional relationship with nature, men and women recognize the importance of water and air management to our traditional communities. The ethics of not taking more than you need from nature is a moral code. Perhaps this explains why earth, forest, rivers wind and other national objects are traditionally believed to be both natural and divine. The philosophy behind this belief may not necessarily be religious but a natural means by which the human environment can be preserved the ethics of care is essential to traditional understanding of environmental protection and conservation.[7]

By ethics of care Ogumgbemi meant an orientation in which one is not taking more than one's needs from nature. However, Ogumbeni is quick to note that this moral code is not unique to African societies as it has a universal appeal and applications, and that there are some interlocking questions that may obliterate its sensibility, justification and adoption in contemporary African order. Pertinent among these questions are. How do we know how much we need, given, the nature of human greed and insatiability? Who judges whether we have been taking more or less than need from the natural resources? If we have been taking more than we need, what are the penalties and how fair are they?

The fundamental questions raised by Ogungein are quite strong and as a consequence, he attempted a reformulation of the traditional environmental practices of *Ethnic of care* in order to make it applicable to contemporary African situation. This conceptual reformulation pale into what Ogunigbemi called *ethics of nature- relatedness*. According to him, ethics of nature relatedness asserts that our natural resources do not need man for their existence and function. the ethics of nature relatedness can be succinctly stated as an ethic that leads human beings to seek to co-exist peacefully with nature and treat it with some reasonable concern for its worth, survival and sustainability.[8]

In Ogumgbemi's submission, ethics of nature relatedness has three basic elements; reason, experience and the will. It does not attribute natural resources to a spiritual nature nor does the creation of natural resources have any religious affinity. With this new ethical thinking, Ogumbemi's expectation is that our present reckless use of nature can be put into order.

In addition to this environmental ethic he envisages, offers some practical suggestions on how to mitigate the current environmental crisis in African. One, he suggested the generation, transmission and distribution of solar energy at a reasonable cost as a safety value in reducing African over reliance on fuel wood, coal kerosene, gas, and petrol as source of energy . Two, on the issue of population, Ogumgbem prophesies that when our population has reached an alarming situation nature will invariably apply its brek through volcanoic eruptions, earthquakes etc) and have a drastic reduction on our population growth rate. Three he recommended a turnaround in African's political leadership in order to put in place good policies that are environmental friendly, he urged them to demonstrate the political will that is necessary in reducing the amount of industrial and agricultural wastes and properly dispose of them so that both our industrial and commercial centers as well as our rural areas are safe from air, land and water pollution.

There are some critical problems in Ogungbemi's ideas of environmental crisis in African and his environmental ethics. But before exposing these, let us also see the perspective of Godfery Tangwa on an African orientation in environmental ethic

Eco Bio Communitarian

Tangwa is another Africa philosopher that has made some reflections and contributions towards creating philosophical awareness on the need for an ethic of the environment in Africa. In his paper: *Some African Reflections on Biomedical and Environmental ethics*, Tangwa bases his conception of an African orientation in environmental ethnic on the metaphysical outlook of pre- colonial traditional African societies, which he called *eco-bio communitaiarian*[9]

This metaphysical world view involves the recognition and acceptance of inter-dependence and peaceful co-existence between earth plants animals and humans. This metaphysical outlook underpinned the ways, manners and cosmic relations between human and his fellow humans. It is also responsible for why traditional Africans were more cautious in their altitude to plants animals and inanimate things and the various invisible forces of the world. True to Tangwa, traditional Africans were more disposed towards the attitudes of live and let live. Tangwa emphasis further that the traditional Africa metaphysical dichotomy between "plants animals and inanimate things, between the sacred and the profane, matter and spirit, the communal and the individual, is a slim and flexible one.[13] it is in line with this metaphysical framework that one can consistently and coherently situate the people's belief in transmigration of the soul into animals, plants or into forces such as the wind. On the basis of this metaphysical understanding of nature and the nature of man Tangwa says such a mindset has a very significant implication for the way nature is approached and treated by traditional Africans. Illustrating his positions on the conciliating relation between human and the environment in tradition African culture, Tangwa cited the stance of his own culture, the Nso in Cameron, According to him, the view of the Nso attitude towards nature and the rest of creation is that of respectful co-existence, conciliation and containment, there are frequently offerings of sacrifices to God, to the divine spirits, both benevolent and malevolent, to the departed ancestors and to the sundry invisible and inscrutable forces of nature.[10]

In all these, the point of Tangwa is that African culture is not against technology whole handsomely, but consistent with cautious and piecemeal use of technology. And given the respect for natural human values that adorn traditional African culture, there are some lessons to be learnt by western culture that has subjected such values to the caprice of the good of technology, industrialization and capitalism.

What is more opposite for Tangwa is that there is nothing wrong with the technology in and of itself but only with the motivation for its development and the uses to which it is put. He condemns the motivation for development of Western technology and the uses to which it has been put which he identified as the will to possess and dominate the world. In his submission, a more humble motivation for the pursuit of science and technology based on the eco-bio-communitarian attitude of live and let live can be substituted for the aggressive motivation of domination to the immeasurable advantage of the whole of mankind.

Commenting on the African perspective to environmental ethnic of both Ogungbeim and Tangwa, is necessary. This is because there are points of disagreements between the two even though they both try to bring to fore solutions to the peculiar African environment crisis. According to P.Ojomo of the Lagos State University, Ogungbemi proposed a reconstructed return to the traditional attitude reflected in the ethnics of care, regarding our interactions with the environment led him to what he termed ethics of nature relatedness. This ethnic of nature relatedness is not a preservationist approach nor is it in any way no anthropocentric. It does not even imply, as he observes, "that natural resources actually have a spiritual nature rather it is an approach that reorganizes that humans necessarily rely upon the natural world for existence because of this reliance, we must treat the environments in which we live with respect for the sake of current and future human well being. One major problem with Ogungbem's ethics of nature relatedness is that it bears little affinity with African cultural belief system. Though Ogungbeim's discourse shows a good understanding of African dimension of the environmental crisis, especially with his analysis of the traditional and modern African societies' contribution to the complexity of the environmental crisis, his position on the needed environmental ethic is alienation of the African spirit and peculiar experiences.[12]

Quite true, as he states, environmental problem in African and anywhere else is primary a consequence of human action. And as value systems inform our actions, we need to search for a viable environmental ethics that is in agreement with African ontology. this is essential in order to pave way for environmental policies that will be compliant with the historic culture experiences of the people and barriers to sustainable green environment. In fact, Ogungbeim's alarming recommendation that nature should invariably apply its brake through volcanic eruptions earthquakes and others in order to have a drastic reduction in African population growth rate is reflective of the disconnectedness of his ethics of nature relatedness and African ontology.

The above mark of deficiency in Ogunbem's ethics of nature relatedness is the strong point of Tangwa's environmental ethics of eco-in-communitarian. Though not without its own problems, the merit of Tangwa's position is that he reorganized the indispensability of African metaphysics in the construction of a meaningful African environmental ethnics. The absence of the dichotomy between plants, animals and inanimate things, between the sacred and the profane, matter and spirit, the communal and the individual in the African metaphysical worldview informed the traditional African disposition and attitude of live and let live. Such metaphysics is not one of domination instigated by greed nor is it consumerist in nature. Latent in that metaphysics are folkloric ascertains and certain taboos that are conservational of iconological balance of the environment. The problem with Tangwa's exploration of an African environmental ethics is that it is an ethno-philosophical defense of indigenous African treatment and management of the environment. He never reorganized the ways and manners by which traditional African contributed to the degradation of the environment albeit ignorance and poverty. This is the strong and commendable point explicit in Ogungbemis position.

In the account of both Ogungbemi and Tangwo, some fundamental questions, which are ethically essential to a plausible African orientation in environmental ethnics, are left upraised let alone discussed and this shall form the concept we seek to pursue in this work such questions as what should be the nature of human obligation and role in the relationship between humans and nature? How can the human person which has a pride of place in African thought system be fitted nonanthropocentrically into African environmental discourse? What is the need for an environmental ethics that is African in orientation? And must such be exclusionary of the existing known environmental theories from the west? What are the political, cultural, economic educational legal and moral imperatives to be taken into consideration in the construction of an African environmental ethnics in order to salvage the African environment from further deteriorations? The solution to environmental destabilization is not purely technological or exclusively attitudinal. Environmental ethics no matter how grounded in African experience it could be or intellectually sophisticated it could be can't alone solve the environmental crisis in Africa. There has to be an orientation that keeps in minds the various imperatives as mentioned above.

We will in the next subheading look at other relational environmental theories as put forward by Ramose, Behrens etc. This will be in line with our commitment to look at some of the African environmental theories put forward and see their strengths and weaknesses before we try to put forward a plausible interpretation of an African non-anthropocentric environmentalism. It is worthy of note that these theories by Ogungbemi and Tangwa are all attempts at positing a non-anthropocentric interpretation of African attitude to the Environment.

Ecology through Ubuntu

Mogobe B. Ramose wrote a brilliant article to articulate African conception or attitude to the environment in the article he tittled *ecology through Ubuntu*.[13] He posited that Motho ke motho ka Batho is a Sotho proverb found in almost all these indigenous languages of African. It means that to be human is to affirm one's humanity reorganizing the humanity of others and on that basis establish human relations with them. Accordingly, it is Botho (Humanness or humanity) and a humane, respectful and polite attitude towards other human beings which constitute the proverbs core or central meaning.[21] Neither the single individual nor the community can define and pursue their respective purposes without recognizing their mutual foundedness, their complementary natures. Wholeness is the regulative principle here since what is asserted is that the single individual is incomplete without the other.

The concept of Batho or Ubuntu, as it is referred to by Ramose in indigenous African languages is not readily translatable into humanism, especially if humanism is understood as a specific trend in on the evolution of western philosophy. Humaneness for him is a better rendition of the concept. According to Ramose, humanness suggests both a condition of being and the states of becoming, of openness or ceaseless unfolding. It is thus opposed to any ism" including humanism for this tends to suggest a condition of finality, a closeness or a kind of absolute either incapable of or resistant to, any further movement.[14] But motion being the principle of change it follows that resistance to motion is tantamount to resistance to change. Ramos avers that this basic difference between humanness and humanism speaks to two difference perceptions of and perspective on, reality or being. Humanness regards being, or the universe, as a complex wholeness involving the multi layered and incessant interaction of all entities. This condition of permanent, multi- directional movement of entities is not by definition chaos. On the contrary, it is both the source and the manifestation of the intrinsic order of the universe. Herein lies. The ecosophical dimension of the indigenous African concept of Ubuntu

The principle of wholeness applies also to the relation between human beings and physical or objective nature. For Ramose, to care for one another, therefore implies caring for physical nature as well. Without such care, the interdependence between human beings and physical nature would be undermined. Moreover human beings are indeed an intrinsic part of physical nature although possibly a privileged part.[23] The point Ramose tries to show is that humans are parts of the whole of nature but having a special place. Accordingly, caring for one another is the fulfillment of the natural duty to care for physical nature too. The concept of harmony in African thought is comprehensive in the sense that it conceives of balance in terms of the totality of the relations that can be maintained between and among human beings as well as between human begins and physical nature. The quest for harmony is thus the striving to maintain a comprehensive but specific relational condition among organism and entities. It is the continuous striving to strike and then maintain a balance between human beings and physical nature.

The loss of Ubuntu for Ramose is compensated for by the somewhat disconsolate comfort and easy life brought about by technological advancement continues to reaffirm the need to restore Ubuntu because more than ever before, humanity is faced with the threat of catastrophic ecological disaster. This is exemplified by widespread air pollution, climate change, the destruction of the ozone layers and the ever constant threat of nuclear ommcide. Botho can make a significant contribution according to Ramose to the quest for universal peace now threatened by nuclear war, however remote such a war may seem. As is widely understood, while nuclear war would reduce the planet to a radioactive rubble, any nuclear accident would have far reaching ecological consequences. The threat of nuclear war represents a water shed in thought on war and peace as it underline the fundamental irrationality of resorting to such a method of warfare. Thus it simultaneously enjoins not only would be nuclear belligerents but also all human kind to seek for peace and build a solid foundation for the construction of peaceful relations among human kind to seek for peace.

Parental Earth Ethics

Ecophilosophy can provide a practical basis upon which to formulate a new ethics that would take into accounts the complexity and totality of nature. This Oruka and Jumia calls this *parental earth ethics.*[14] Parental earth ethics is not simply of intellectual enquiry. It is the basis upon which different cultures around the world including Africa would base their environmental perception. This ethics can be presented on the form of principles and rules.

Imagine families with six children, two of the six are relatively rich and four generally poor. Among the rich, one is extremely rich while among the poor, three are very poor. The reason for the difference in status have to do partly with the family history, partly with personal luck and partly with individual talents. Though the children have different and diverse possessions, they have certain things in common such as parents (whether alive or diseased) they are also common in that each of them has status and achievements based on the teaching which the family as a whole provided. Some made better use of that while others may have squandered it.

The children find that their lives and relationships are guided by the unwritten ethical laws which can best be summarized under two main principles (i) Parental debt (or bond) Principle (pp) and (ii) individual luck principal.[15]

Parental Debts Principle

This principle according to Oruka and Jumia, consists of four related rules dealing with family, security and dignity, parental debt, and individual and family survival. The family security rules states that the fate and security (Physical or welfare) of each member of a family is ultimately bound up with the existential reality of the family, as a whole. Any one of the six members may for example, be arrogant and have enough to claim self- sufficiency and independence from the rest, However, eventually, the person and the person's own progeny may experience a turn of events which could make them desperately in need of protection from the family.

History abounds with such example; both the Roman and the Otoman Empire disintegrated and their children and dependents sought their security and fate elsewhere. Western Europe was liberated from economic rain after the Second World War by a power outside her borders And today, the former soviet Union is desperately looking for rescue from such a small power as Italy.

The kinship shame rule is that the life condition of any member of the family affect all the others materially and emotionally, as no member can be proud of his or her situation however happy, if any member of the family tree lives in squalor. There is a partial non earthen application of this rule in our current world. European powers are more inclined to help fellow Europeans out of their squalor than they are prepared to do the same for some third world country. The parental debt rule assumes and explains the relationship and debt between the family members. Whichever member is affluent or destitute owes his fortune or misfortune to the parental and historical factors inherent on the development of the family. Hence within the family, no one above is fully res possible neither for his affluence nor for his misfortune.

The individual and family survival rule states that no member of the family given the above rules has any moral obligation to refrain from interfering with the possession of any brother or sister who ignores the obligation to abide by the rules of the family ethics. This rule allows the disadvantaged to demand assistance from the affluent but it also allows the creative and the hardworking members of the family to repossess underdeveloped possessions of the idle relatives and develop them for use of posterity the individual lack principle.

This is made up of three constituent rules according to Oruka etal, dealing with personal achievements, personal supererogation, and public law. The personal achievement rule states that what a member passes is due mainly to the person's special talents. This is a kind of family individualism which disregards historical experience and the organic constitution of the family. The personal supererogation rule provides that every member has a right to do whatever he or she wishes with his or her possession. Finally the family public laws stales that any member of the family who contravenes the right of another member as given by the second principle will be subject to the family public law, and would be punished or reprimanded and ordered to restore justice. The parental debt principle takes precedence over the individual lack principle in case of a conflict between the two. And this is all it should be. Why, for example, would we not see it as senseless that an individual member of a family would want to do anything she wishes with her possessions, while a member of her kids or kin may be in desperate need of help? The basic ethical rationale for why the parental debt principle takes precedence is as follows, the individual luck principle (P) is supported fundamentally by the "right of first occupation, personal luck and achievements. I.e. The veil of fate but the first principle (PP} springs from the fact of organic unity between the children, the common pool of their wealth (whatever the differences in possessions) and the need for the common security. The ethics of common sense shows that when in any given family or community matters of common wealth, and common security conflict with matters of the personal possession; lack or achievements, the former must prevail over the later.

There is no country, he argues, in which for example, an individual institution would be safe guarded if it endangers the security or the economy of all the nations. And it is also clear that no country would accept the wish or a will from one of its citizens which stipulates that upon death, all his achievements, however dear to the country, should be exterminated or kept out of use by anybody. The reason for such a will would be that those achievements are personal and hence, the personal superogation rule is to prevail. The objection to this will can only be supported by involving the issue of common origin, common security and common wealth. It is clear for this, that the earth or the world is s kind of a family unit in which the members have kith and kin relationship with one another, so far our discussion is driven towards the claim that the earth is a common wealth to all humanity.

We are prepared to concede that the world has no sovereign. But this does not affect the claim that planet earth not the world is a common good or heritage for all humankind. The question of the right by first occupation or personal achievement does not overrule this truth. If it did, then it would make no sense to accept the territorial rights of the Europeans who migrate to America after Christopher Columbus discovered that continent over five hundred years ago.

The territorial rights and sovereignty in the Americas would in that case rightly and legitimated belong to the indigenous Indians. However the reality today is such that indigenous Indians have no more a legitimate claim to that part of the earth than the migrants who invaded it five hundred years ago. Again if the rights of first occupation or generally the veil of fate is to prevail over the principle of the earth as a common good for all humankind then all that was procured through the colonization of such places like Africa and India should have been returned to these former colonies a long time ago. But nowadays, it seems it does not make sense to demand that such resources be returned. On colonialism, what we lament is the fact that those who developed themselves by it have turned their backs on those they colonized and now claim that they (the former subjects) have no share in or claim to any of their current possession. But given the organic constitution of life and the principle of parental earth ethics the former colonies have a legitimate claim to such possession.

Oruka etal tried to argue for their position. For them an objection may arise from this submission. One such objection would be that earth is not a common good in the sense of sharing whatever we have gained from it with everybody. The earth is a common good only in the sense that is an open field for the survival of the fittest.[16] The third, Reich of Hitler was to last 1000 years. But it lasted for only 12 years. The Roman employee of course lasted a long time, but it did not last forever. Today, the descendants of (say) the British Empire would surely feel some relief and pride in any historical revelation of any good which the enquire did to the colonies for it is precisely from the goods not the evils done by colonization that makes former subjects tolerant and at time even friendly to their former oppressors.

So when we take not the subservient ends of nations, but the ultimate or organic ends of all nature, no particular species or nation could be the fittest or weakest in accordance with the historical organic shifts of nature. Perhaps what all nations which are rich and powerful need to do is to invest in the pool of the rest of the world, so that when their historical turn or shift to oblivion comes, others may remember them with compassion. This would be a parental earth insurance policy. The other objection is that parental earth ethic is a quasi-religious exaggeration of the kinship relationship between all people of the earth, that is it is a doctrine for preachers in churches but not relevant to the real world of the political and economic class bond.

The kinship issue is not being dragged into this matter just as moralizations of the virtue of declaring all human beings, and all species in nature as "brothers and sisters" Ii is given here as an assertion derived from the ecological truth about nature and the ultimate common fate of all creatures living on planet earth. Without the element of kinship or organic unity of nature none of the arguments of the current environmental protectionist would be valid for all peoples and nations. But given the organic unity of nature, the arguments make sense for it is clear that the pollution and the degradation of sections of the earth are likely to have consequence in the rest of the globe. This is the concern that led to the convening of the earth submit in Brazil in 1992. The meeting was a symbol of family gathering.

The last objective is one which claims that we are placing creatures such as even earthworm in the same moral level as human beings. Equality of all human beings may be understandable, but how about equality (say) between a head of a state and an earthworm? The earthworm does not demand or require equality with a head of state but nature demands that we do not extinguish earthworm specie. Earthworms are a part of the biodiversity without which even a head of state would be non-existent.

There are basically two main reasons in the need for the sustenance of biodiversity. One is that all sentient- being has an intrinsic value and the other is that human life on earth is doomed to perish if we destroy biodiversity. Although the first reason is still too remote for most people to grasp, the second reason is and should be today common knowledge any reasonable adult human beings. We propose parental earth ethics as a basic ethic that would offer a motivation for both a global environment concern and a global redistribution of the wealth of nations.

Let us now look at African relational environmentalism. It has some similarities with Parental Earth Ethics, and Ubuntu ecology as all focus on themes like: relationships, interdependence interconnectedness and interrelatedness. The whole world in an African understanding is interconnected with each other. A harm to one aspect like the physical nature will have a strong effect on rest of the ecosystem and this informs human relationship with her environment. The second point of similarity in these theories on African environmentalism in the place it accords man. They see man as a privileged part of nature (Ubuntu) or as a being in whom relating with counts. Such that the more close or cordial the relationship with man is the more moral status will be accorded. They also pride themselves as being devoid of ethnocentric. Let us now look at African Relational environmental

African Relational Environmentalism

Relational theory in African ethical discourse was first put forward by an American born philosopher. Thaddeus Metz. This he did in his intelligent article titled. *An African Theory of Moral Status. A Relational Alternative to individualism and Holism.*[17] This view argues that animals and humans both have moral status that is of the same kind but different in degree; in the sense that even a severely mentally incapacitated human being has a greater moral stats than an animal with identical internal properties and a new born in fact has a greater moral status than a mid – to- late stage foetus. He argues too that the Holists accord no moral status to any of these beings assigning it only to groups to which they belong, while individualists such as welfares grant an equal moral status either to animal or severally mentally incapacitated humans. Relational theory of moral status therefore argues that it does a better job of accounting for degrees of moral status. Thus according to Metz, something has moral status in so far as it is capable of having a certain causal or intentional connection with another being.

This view is grounded in salient sub-Saharan moral views roughly according to which the greater a being's capacity to be part of a communal relationship with us the greater its moral status. I understand this theory to be purely African in a great sense. The more relationship is closer to human the more moral status it has. This therefore implies that a goat has better, moral status than a rat, it also implies that a mad man still has a stronger moral status than a goat because of the status of the relationship.

This theory has been criticized especially by Horthenske, in his *Animal and African Ethic* as anthropocentric. For him, it is human centered to judge moral considerability based on relationship with humans in particular. Otherwise why should it be humans whose close relationship with, confers moral status.[18] the researcher understands Metz work to be strongly based on Africa ontology at least English speaking Africa. This relational conception can also be seen in theories like Ubuntu Ecology. Ubuntu argues that all things interrelate but that humans are a privileged part of the relationship even though Romose failed to give the sense in which humans are privileged. This can therefore make the argument that the privilege accorded man in Ubuntu is anthropocentric.. The second strong importance of the three theories; Ubuntu, parental earth ethics and rotational theory is that they are somewhat not ethnocentric. They do not base their arguments on the ancestors, gods, spirits and those ethnocentric insinuation that in my view do not pass for professional philosophy. One can assert the ontology of particular society but philosophy demands that we do not just stop at a sociological religious interpretation of being in societies but sieve out philosophical critical perspectives that is universalizable and that can pass for real philosophy otherwise it came only pass for ethnophilosphy. I hereby applaud the sense in which Ubuntu, parental earth ethics and Relational moral status posit their theories. Nevertheless I argue here that if we extend this relational moral status to the environment like Kevin Behrens did few problems will emerge that will tilt the theory towards anthropocentrism.

Behrens Kelvin after citing few examples of works of African philosophers that posited the interrelated and inter connectedness of being, posited what he called African relational environmentalism.[19] His project was to articulate if possible, a promising non-anthropocentric

African theory as a counter to the anthropocentric view of philosophers. According to him, some philosophers like Callicott, Bujo, Tempels has claimed erroneously that African ontology favour anthropocentrism. He therefore posited that contrary to anthropocentric ideas that there is a strong emphasis on the interrelatedness or interconnectedness of human beings and the rest of nature that is also evident in African thought providing basis for a promising African environmentalism.

According to many African theorists, the belief in the interdependence of natural entities clearly implies that people should respect and live in harmony with the community of nature. The robustly communitarian character of much African ethic informs this moral requirement to live in harmony, individual members of the community of nature can be fulfilled only in and though their relationship with others. These relationships are often characterized in familial terms, emphasizing the need for mutual support solidarity, care and nurturing. I have suggested elsewhere that this approach to the environmentalism holds promise for environmental ethics because of its relational focus. This is what Behrens calls *African relational environmentalism.*[42] he avers that on this relational approach virtue is achieved through maintaining harmonious relationships that prioritize neither the individual nor the community while respecting both. Since the interest and needs of both individual and groups always count, and always need to be kept in balance, this approach is able to avoid the extreme of both individualism and holism.

In developing this non anthropocentric African Relational Environmentalism further, Behrens also tried to establish what kind of things might plausibly, be considered to be part of the community of nature and capable of being included in this familial or communal relationship. Since on this African approach, harmonious relationships with other natural entities ought for be nurtured. In defining what should constitute the community or what should be morally considerable, Behnens tries to differentiate between moral status and moral considerability. For him, moral status could mean just respecting and promoting a being but moral considerability is much more. In the literature of environmental philosophy, the notion moral considerability is quite often used interchangeably with the notion of moral value. But the two notions are not exactly the same. Moral value is something that ought to be protected and/or promoted. But to say that something has moral considerability is to say that its existence wellbeing interest preference and or some other aspects of it ought to be directly rather than indirectly given positive weight in our moral deliberations about action that are likely to affect it. Hence while things are mostly considerable, it is not necessarily the other way round.

Thus Behrens identified few factors that confer moral considerability; life, sentience and rationality. He also identified few factors that confer moral considerability in African though system, example interrelatedness, life force, totemism, inhabit spirit and folklore etc. Behrens agues however that if one understands life as existing in individual things as well as in an interconnected web, then this African view may well be described as life – centered approached. To distinguish it from more conventional biocentric or life centered approaches, he refer to this view as "web of life centered"[20] For him, what grants moral considerability or constitutes community to an entity is not that it has an individual life telos of its own but that it is part of the web or fabric of life. And then on this view all things that can be part of this web of life that themselves share or enable this life can be morally considerable. Since everything that forms part of the web is in some way interconnected or interdependent with other parts of the web, all these entities need to be taken into account morally. Hence Behrens asserted that most plausible interpretation of the various overlapping conceptions of moral considerability in African thought is that they ground moral considerability in being part of the interconnected web of life.

In essence Behrens' African relational environmentalism and Thad Metz' relational theory differs in some subtle sense, while moral standing or moral considerability is granted to being the closer they relate to human, Behrens view of moral status is web of life centre entity. This means in my views a broader perspective. While Metz's concept of African moral considerability is being that relates more closely to humans, Behrens conception is somewhat holistic. I see in Metz's conception a purely African understanding of moral standing in so far as humans in African context have a pride of place. Also Metz concept of modal relation answer deeper question as regards moral standing of a fetus, mad woman, and other serious ethical puzzles. Nevertheless here is a sense in which philosophers like Horthenske would see relational theory as anthropocentric. Modal relational theory distinguished humans form the rest of the ecosystem in the sense that it is relationship with Human that should confer moral stand. Horthnske would ask, why not relationship with animals like dog or lizard? I see Metz as asserting the in African at least English speaking sub. Saharan African humans has a stake, a strong stake in the whole of ecosystem, same view was reiterated by Ramose when he posited a holistic view of the ecosystem but did not forget to say that human are a privileged part, even though it is part of the whole ecosystem. How then do we describe this human place? Failure to give the sense in which humans participate in this whole drama will simply be termed anthropocentric. This paper therefore sets out to attempt a non- anthropocentric sense of asserting the place of human in the ecosystem.

Humans have a place in the ecosystem and such place is not right based where humans have the legal or whatever right to kill, eat and dominate the world, rather it is a place; an obligatory place, a task based, job oriented place. It is humans who should take responsibility for the whole of ecosystem. I intend in the next section to discuss a view I call obligatory anthropoholism. This is a plausible African conception of our attitude to the environment. The views discussed above are all in one way or the other throwing light and clarifying views on African environmentalism, but giving just a holistic approach, in my view does not just answer the question of who tends or who should work the other. Also highlighting the place of humans giving a sense in which humans have this place, distinguishing it from the old anthropocentric view begs the question. I seek to assert and subtly too, that humans have a place in the whole of ecosystem. This holistic picture offered by African philosophers cannot be complete without highlighting the place of man. Second highlighting the place of man without giving the sense in which humans have this place is also incomplete.

Obligatory Anthropoholism; A Plausible African Perspective to the Environment.

The theory I wish to pursue as a plausible alternative to these theories should be one that will have the following characteristics firstly, it should show mastery of African ontology. Thereby being African enough. Secondly it should highlight holism as an important aspect of Africa ontology which informs our relationship to the environment. Thirdly, it should in some sense be my view that is my individual conception of what an African environmental ethics should be, being informed and also standing on the view of other African environmental ethicists. This way, I shall be held accountable for my flaws, misinterpretations and misappropriation of other concepts and not hide under the cloak of African ontology to make submission. I am of the view that individualism in this light is not pride but humility and accepting to be criticized and corrected if need be. Fourthly, the theory I wish to pursue should have and retain a special, privileged place for humans in line with African ontology. This pride of place has been the subject of misunderstanding in African environmental ethics as it is often branded anthropocentric. It is worthy of note here that African ontology has that place for man from Tempels, Ogotemeli, Ubuntu, Uwa ontology, Ife and Onye ontology, Relational moral status etc. fifthly and more importantly, there should be a sense in which humans are a privileged part in the holistic ecosystem.

This sense brings to fore the non-anthropocentric understanding of African environmental attitude. This portends that even though humans are a privileged part of the ecosystem, it cannot be interpreted as anthropocentric. Sixthly, I will give an application of my theory into real environmental issues like Ekwulobia erosion at Oko and Ekwulobia Nigeria and attempt using the theory to try resolving this environmental menace.

I call my view to African environmental theory Obligatory anthropoholism. This underscore both the place of man (Anthropos) the holistic concept of being in Africa, whereby all existing things intercompenetrates each other (Holism) and I give a sense in which humans are singled out of the whole. This sense is the facts of obligation. It is human who is under obligation to care for the whole of ecosystem. I am writing because I wish to prescribe to humans and not cows, how to relate, care, tend and conserve the ecosystem. This is practical and simple; humans' special place is not a right bussed placement, which is somewhat alien to Africa. It is in the light of the capacity for obligation that humans are privileged. Right based conception is what brought anthropocentrism, Obligation based ethics will strike a balance in the whole of ecosystem.Most act-oriented ethical reasoning looks at required action, not rights, and at obligation, rather than at preferred outcome. Act-centred ethics, in its many forms seek to establish certain principles of obligations which are to constrain not only individual action but institutions and practices. .

The great advantage of rights-based ethics is that it is so beautifully adapted to making claims; its great disadvantage is that these claims can be made with flourish and bravado while leaving it wholly obscures who, if anyone has a duty or obligation to meet them. Yet if nobody has obligation that correspond to a supposed right, then, however loudly it is claimed or proclaimed, the right amounts to nothing. Proclaiming rights is all too easy; taking them seriously is another matter, and they are not taken seriously unless the corollary obligations are identified and taken seriously. Although the rhetoric of rights has become the most widely used way of talking about justice in the last fifty years, it is the discourse of obligations that addresses the practical question who ought to do what for whom?

The profound structural difficulties of the discourse of rights can be obscured because many discussions of rights veer unconsciously between claims about fundamental natural or moral rights and claims about institutional or positive rights. Identifying the obligations which are the counterparts to institutionalized or positive rights is unproblematic: here the move back to practical discourse is easily achieved. However, appeals to institutional and positive rights are not justification of those rights: institutional and positive rights are objects rather than the sources of ethical criticisms and justification. In some societies some humans have had the positive rights of slave- masters; in others bear who kill or maim other animals have had positive rights to a trial. Neither fact establishes anything about the justice or the ethical acceptability of slavery or about the capacities of bears to act wrongly or unjustly, or their rights to due process. To establish what is right or wrong, just or unjust, right-based reasoning would have to appeal to fundamental, moral or natural rights- yet these are the very right whose counterpart obligations can so easily be over-looked, with the consequences that they are merely proclaimed and not taken seriously, and that a theoretical rather than a practical approach to ethics is adopted.

These are ample reasons for act-oriented ethical reasoning to take obligations rather than rights as basic. A switch of perspective from recipience to action, from rights to obligations, carries no theoretical costs and may yield considerable gain: a focus on obligations will incorporate everything that can be covered by a focus on rights (since any genuine right must be matched by a converse obligation) and can also incorporate any other less tightly specified obligations, which lack counterpart rights.

Moreover, this switch of focus from rights to obligations is productive for environmental ethics; the main advantage of taking obligations as basic is simple gain in clarify about obligatory Anthropoholism. Even if some rights are not human rights, all obligations will be human obligations. Or, putting the matter more carefully, obligations can be held and discharged only where capacities for action and for reasoning reach a certain degree of complexity, and we have no knowledge of such capacities except among human beings and in institution created and staffed by human being. And so in obligatory Anthropoholism, humans, having a pride of place in Africa are only defined in terms of their obligatory role to the environment. It is humans as agents who will care for the holistic ecosystem.

Same view can justify an anthropocentric approach but I think the slight difference is the fact that in obligatory anthropoholism, the obligation is not targeted at just human ends, for human benefit or for his economic enrichment, rather the African concept of holism; the interrelatedness, interconnectedness, intercompentraion between both the seen and the unseen elements puts humans under obligation to tend, care and conserve the environment. It is nonanthropocentric when we look at the end to which obligatory anthropoholism aims. The chief end or purpose for anthropocentrism is human benefit but not so for obligatory anthropoholism, the purpose or telos end for which obligatory anthropoholism aims is holistic, the whole of ecosystem, humans are just the agent which can simply fulfill this end. Thus, I propose that African environmental philosophy seen from this light provides a promising nonanthropocentric, practical and very simplistic approach to the environmental concerns of both Africa and the world at large

Few objections and criticisms can be made against obligatory anthropoholism in my view; the first is that it is anthropocentric because it makes humans the agent of obligation and sees human from a privileged perspective. This by implication will make humans exploit rather than tend the environment, at the end of the day, we are back to anthropocentrism again. Secondly, there can be criticisms about its Africanness, where scholars have argued that African environmental perspective is simply anthropocentric. Thirdly, is the question of how this theory can comfortably fit into the issues and challenges in the African soil, fight and defeat them.

In attempting but not exhausting these criticisms, it is worthy of note that mine is only an attempt at evolving an Africa theory of environmentalism that can match and defeat the challenges of the environment in Africa and elsewhere, my theory does not boast of mastery, it does not in any way dismiss or counter the views or themes of other Africa environmentalist it is only a humble contribution to the understanding of Africa environmentalism. As much as possible, it is a personal understanding made out of African ontology, it therefore cannot be said to authoritatively assume "the African environmental approach". The implication of the above statement is that it puncturable, it can be criticized and can be built upon; it is a contribution among other contribution which does not claim to exhaust all there is to African environmental philosophy. This position is really worthy of note for critics of obligatory Anthropoholism.

In reply to the first criticism of obligatory anthropoholism being anthropocentric and thereby falling into the pit it has tried to fill up, it is important for me as well as for all to understand that for whatever position you choose to take anthropocentric, nonanthropocentric and ecocentric, the humans are the one who will still be the agent is all these discourse. Humans are the ones who should care for the whole of ecosystem, they are the ones we are writing to, they are the ones who should be obligated to protect the ecosystem, whether as institution or as parastatals, action based ethics can justify anthropocentric ethics but can also justify Africa obligatory anthropoholism. The simple difference in African obligatory anthropoholism is that the purpose and end (telos) of humans obligation is African ontology is interconnectedness, togetherness and this fulfills her humanness as Ramose asserts, it is in working for the betterment of all both humans and physical nature that the human in Ubuntu finds fulfillment and satisfaction. It is in respectful relationship with the environment that eco-bio communitarian of Tangwa finds satisfaction.

It is that relationship defined from the obligatory role that makes African relational environmentalism worthwhile. It is the obligatory role of humans to the environment that makes it necessary to assert as Metz does, that it is relating with humans that somewhat confers moral status. The implication of this theory is germane, the humans has a pride of place in African ontology and this place is the place of obligation to care for not just herself in the sense of using the physical nature for personal gains but rather in holistic sense of being the one who enforce holism. This means in practical terms that man should eat cow, goat, also means that humans should protect rivers and the atmospheric air for the sake of the circle of ecosystem and since the end is holism, it differs from anthropocentrism. The purpose of anthropocentrism is human benefit, the while the purpose of obligatory anthropoholism is ecocentric or holistic.

In the end, all theories if seen from an obligatory action perspective will come back to an agent (humans) and thus nonanthropocentric view can as well be justifiable with this. On the question of the Africanness of obligatory anthropoholism, a theory in African environmental philosophy is African the extent to which it imbibes the values extracted from African ontology. It therefore requires a theorist to show mastery of African ontology Given, ethnophilosophy or what Prof. Innocent Asousu calls unintended ethnocentric commitments may question the criticality of some African ontology for instance, arguments from ancestors, deities and gods. Asousu posits that these sociological or cultural postulations are simply not philosophical because of two reasons, firstly, they are not critical or rational and secondly, some of these philosophers hide under African communal thought to express their individuality, oftentimes seen as overgeneralization. Philosophy trives in individuality and not communal thought.

I argued elsewhere however, that even though African ontological discourse of some philosophies are ethnocentric, they are raw materials for philosophy and necessary tool for evolution of a promising African environmental ethics. This is true in the sense that it is from African experience, ideologies, worldviews and cosmologies that a promising African philosophy can be formed, since going outside the African experience will not foster or motivate Africans effectively to care for their environment, scholars like Hargrove will suggest that theorists should enrich their theories with the peculiarities of their different cultures so as to motivate and persuade men and women to care for their environment. African ontology holds values such as togetherness, holism and a special place for man high. And it is based on these values when well interpreted that a promising environmental nonanthropocentric philosophy can emerge. Obligatory anthropoholism inculcates these values example humans, holism and also gives the sense in which human being is privileged.

As to how this theory can be comfortable applied into the African peculiar environmental situation, obligatory anthropoholism is not a complex theory but a simple practical one. The factors involved are simple humans and enlightenment as to the best practices as regards to environmental protection. At Ekwulobia and Oko, serious gully erosion has greatly affected the land at different sides. These erosions are not just one but many. There is this superstitious belief that a god called Ududo Nka who is a big python, is responsible for the erosion and continues to open it once it is provoked by the natives. Obligatory anthropoholism will simply task the human around to protect first the rest of the land by planting trees and crops and not falling trees. The theory blames humans and not the goddess nor the ecosystem. The theory is not ethnocentric and therefore does not thrive in superstition.

It blames humans because of their incessant falling of bush trees to build houses for themselves without adequate replacement and care for the land thereby leaving the soil porous to be overrun by flood. It posits that humans should be adequately educated as to the ecosystem and the implication of obstructing the circle of ecosystem causing erosion thereby. If such menace will be prevented, humans have a role to play. Government is however beckoned to help out as the natives can only prevent further occurrence but not control the heavy gully erosion already in existence. Obligatory anthropoholism conceives that if adequate enlightenment be given, even to the uneducated on how best to protect the environment, and the reasons why, it will go a long way rather than simply ascribing rights to humans, animals and land.

Conclusion

Obligatory Anthropoholism has a strong conviction that environmental ehtics or no environmental ethics, Africa should be developed; starting from the human person to infrastructure and to all other spheres of human endevour. Obligatory anthropohohlism does not abdicate the social responsibility of development to only God, the Government or institutions alone; it asserts that all humans have something to add. It also calls on African governments to establish more educational institutions. Here lies the developmental import of obligatory anthropoholism as a plausible non anthropocentric African environmentalism. With adequate enlightenment, even the uneducated can value the environment. With adequate enlightenment, even anthropocentrism will lead humans to care for the environment. Without adequate enlightenment, even nonanthropocentric environmental ethics and obligatory anthropoholism will not be effective as regards environmental conservation. Obilgatory anthropoholism therefore affirms the importance of humans in any developmental concept or approach in Africa.

References

1. *www.conserve-energy-future.com/15 current environemntal problems.php*
2. Ferre Frederick. 'Technology, Ethics and the End of Nature' In H. Odera Oruka (ed) *Philosophy and Ecology; Philosophy of Nature and Environmental Ethics.* (Nairobi, Kenya. ACTS Press, 1994). p. 220
3. Godfrey B. Tangwa. 'Some Reflections on Biomedical and Environmental Ethics' In Kwasi Wiredu (ed), *A Companion to African Philosophy.* (Malden: Blackwell Publishing Ltd, 2004) p.388
4. Ogungbemi, Segun. "An African perspective on the Environmental crisis" In Pojman, Louis J. (ed) *Environmental Ethics. Readings in theory and application*, 2nd ed (Belmont, C.A Wadsworth Publishing Company 1997) p. 330
5. *Ibid p. 204*
6. *Ibid p. 205*
7. *Ibid p. 206*
8. *Ibid p. 207*
9. Tangwa, Godfrey. "Some African Reflection on Biomedical and Environmental Ethics" In Kwasi Wiredu (ed) *A Companion to African philosophy.* (Oxford: Blackwell publishers, 2004) p.385
10. *Ibid p. 389*
11. *Ibid p. 387*

12. P.A Oyomo. "Environmental Ethics: An African understanding", In *the journal of Pan African studies* Vol 4. N0. 3 (Mandi 2011) p. 103

13. Mogobe B Ramose: "Ecology through Ubuntu" In *Journal of African Ethics,* (Harare: Mond Press) p.309

14. H. Odera Oruka and C. Juma. "Ecophilosophy and Parental Earth Ethics" In H. Odera Oruka (ed) *Philosophy, Humanity and Ecology,* (Nairobi: ACTS Press, 1994) p.117

15. *Ibid p 117*

16. *Ibid p. 119*

17. Thaddeus Metz. "An African Theory of Moral Status: A Relational Alterretive to Individualism and Holism" In Robert F. Heeger and Albert W.Musschenga (eds) *Ethical Theory and Moral practice an International Forum.* P. Vol 15. No. 3 (Springer: 2012) p 387

18. Kai Horsthemke. *Animal and African Ethics,* (London: Palgrove Macmillian,2015) p. 15

19. Kelvin Gary Behrens. "An African Relational Environmentalism and Moral Considerability" In Journal of Environment Ethics. (Crossmark: Vol. 36, 2015) P. 64

20. *Ibid. p. 68*

21. *Ibid. p. 70*

CHAPTER FIVE

A METAPHYSICAL EXPISTEMOLOGICAL STUDY OF AFRICAN MEDICAL PRACTITIONERS

KANU, Ikechukwu Anthony

Introduction

In David Hume's treatment of the compatibilism of freedom and necessity, he spoke of things happening by chance, meaning that things could happen without any cause as such. The word 'perchance' is a recurrent one in the works of William Shakespeare, precisely in the 'Twelfth Night', and this reveals the Western understanding that things can happen by chance. For the African, the world is an ordered universe in which all events are caused and potentially explicable. The African does not just speak of mechanical, chemical and psychological interactions like his western counterparts; he also speaks of a metaphysical kind of causality, which binds the creator and the spiritual world to the creature (Egbeke 2001). Through this interaction, a force could weaken or re-enforce another. Each force has an activating principle or vital force which allows it to function in a specific manner.

Egbeke (2001), observes that even when the African speaks of *odachi*, or *Ife mberede*, an accident or the unexpected event, he does not speak in terms of chance, but in terms of an event whose cause is not yet known. This explains why for most Africans, when one is bitten by a snake, it is not just understood as the product of chance, it is interpreted as sorcery or witchcraft. When one sneezes, it is believed that someone is somewhere gossiping about you. Because of the need to trace the causes of these events and conditions, counteract them and appease or punish those behind them, the African employs the help of sacred specialists like the medical practitioners. The burden of this piece is to explore the place and significance of medical practitioners in African life and philosophy.

The Practice of African Medicine

A lot of research has been done in the area of African traditional medicine and the medical practitioners themselves (Maclean 1971, Twumasi 1975, Johada 1977, Ademuwagun 1979, Ityavyar 1982, 1984). Medicine men belong to a class called variously: specialists, sacred personages, special men, sacred men or sacred specialists. They principally concern themselves with sickness, disease and misfortune. They symbolize the hope of society: hopes of good health, security and prosperity. In African traditional societies, sickness, disease and misfortune are generally believed to be caused by the ill will or ill action of one person against the other. The medicine man is thus consulted to diagnose the type of sickness and trace the cause of it. The satisfactory answer that people need at a time when the question of the cause is sought is that 'someone' caused it. Even if it is a mosquito bite, someone must have sent the mosquito. As a solution to the problem in question, the cause must be found, counteracted, uprooted and punished. It is also the duty of the medical practitioner to provide countermeasures that can counteract future inflictions. They are the doctor and pastor of the sick. Mbiti (1969) refers to them as the friends, pastors, psychiatrists and doctors of African traditional societies. As sacred specialists, they have a language, symbolism, knowledge and skill of their own.

Precisely, they are also called traditional doctors or traditional healers, herbalists because they have power and control over herbs (Quarcoopome, 1987), traditional doctors, *Dibia* in Igbo and *Waganga* in Swahili. Unlike the priest who is limited to his or her shrine, the medicine man or woman is mobile. There are times when they keep the sick in their homes and take care of them. There are also times when they visit the sick in their homes, especially when they are not living far away from the medicine man or woman. There are also times when the nature of the sickness determines the place for treatment. Some treatments could only be administered in designated areas of the community. While some are treated in public, others are treated in private. Usually when the cases are still at their lowest levels, the family medicine man or woman takes care of it, but if it does persist, a specialized medical practitioner is consulted (Ityavyar, 1990).

In West African societies, complicated cases such as bewitchment are treated in shrines, pools, isolated hills, thick forests, river deltas, road junctions and other places deemed therapeutically acceptable to the healer and his spiritual friends. Perhaps these places are more convenient for the healers to evoke spirits, converse with them and appease them with appropriate sacrifices. However, just like in the case of a priest, every family has medical personnel that practices half time rather than full time. Full time medical services are provided only by the publicly consecrated medicine men (Ityavyar, 1990). The medical practitioners have an office personality which is not easily accessible to the common villager. This makes the study of them complicated. Because the Europeans who encountered Africa earlier, misunderstood African cultural practices as pagan; it is thus not surprising that African medical practitioners suffered much in their hands and more so in the hands of European-American writers and missionaries who often called them witch-doctors, alongside other derogatory names.

However, Mbiti (1969), observes that medicine men and women are the greatest gift to African societies and the most useful source of help. It is therefore not surprising that every village in traditional Africa has a medicine man within reach. He is accessible to everyone at almost every time and comes into the picture of the people's life as individuals and as a community.

The Call of Medical Practitioners

There are no fixed ways of calling a medical practitioner in Africa. People emerge as medical practitioners through various ways. Neither is there a particular age or season when they are called into the business. One could be called into it during his or her early age or later in life. There is no particular sex required for the work; both men and women can be medical practitioners in Africa. However, Ityavyar (1990) observes that healers in most traditional African societies tend to be adult males, with only very few women who specialize in administering simple cures to child care. The most famous women healers specialize in issues relating to bareness and birth complications. Each community has at least one of such women who have reached the age of menopause. She is always surrounded by young girls who help her. They are believed to posses certain powers through birth or eating certain herbs.

Although the personal qualities of medical differ, Mbiti (1969) observes that they are expected to be trustworthy, morally upright, friendly, willing and ready to serve, able to discern people's needs and not be exorbitant in their charges. Like the priest, medical practitioners are called through apprenticeship, inheritance and extraordinary signs.

Apprenticeship

There are obviously no formal institutions for training of medical practitioners, they learn through observations. And in fact, every medical practitioner no matter how he or she has been called undergoes training. An aging medicine man or woman will normally choose an assistant who is interested in the profession; this could be a close relative or a son who would in due course take after him or her. There are also cases where people make their intentions known to the medicine man or woman of his or her intention to become one. Such a person is carefully scrutinized by the teacher to ascertain that he really means business. Such person's training according to Mbiti (1969), is usually long and expensive. However, Evans-Pritchard (1937) says that payment for the training varies from society to society, and is made from time to time as the candidate continues to acquire knowledge, which may involve learning one medicine for a month or two.

According to Mbiti (1969), candidates acquire knowledge in relation to medicinal value, quality and use of different herbs, leaves, roots, fruits, barks, grasses and of various objects like minerals, dead insects, bones, feathers, powders and smoke from different objects, excreta of animals and insects, shells, eggs etc. These are the elements employed by the medicine man in his services to the people. According to Hammond (1960, p.340), "Among the Modu of South Africa, there is practically no plant whose backs, twigs, roots bulbs or leaves are not at one time or the other pressed into service as an ingredient in some magical connection". The candidate also acquires knowledge as regards the causes, cures and prevention of diseases and other forms of suffering such as barrenness, misfortune, poor crop yield, magic, witchcraft and sorcery and how to combat them; the nature and handling of spirits and the living dead and some other secrets, known only to the inner caucus.

As the candidate continues with the training, Arinze (2008) observes that he undergoes different duties such as errands, household chores, carrying materials for ceremonies and gathering of herbs with and for the master. Such candidates are sometimes given particular marks on their bodies. They have particular attire they wear. They are expected to be totally obedient to their masters and are sometimes expected to be celibate and acetic so as to discipline the mind and body. During the period of training, Mbiti (1969) asserts that each teacher tutors his pupils with his own regulations, for there are no general regulations as such. Regulations could be refraining from eating animals like elephants, house rats and various plants, and from sexual intercourse or bathing for several days after one has eaten certain herbs from the master.

After training, the candidate is, in some societies, formally and publicly initiated into the profession of medical practitioners, so that everyone may recognise the person and his qualification. They even form associations or corporations as in many African societies.

Heredity

One of the ways through which people are called into this class of sacred personalities is through inheritance. In this case, a medical practitioner passes on the profession to a son or a younger relative. In this case, a child usually the first is chosen to take after the father or mother. The person who inherits the office also has to go through some apprenticeship from whomever he or she would succeed (Onuigbo, 2009).

Extraordinary signs

Mbiti (1969) argues that there are medical practitioners called by spirits or the living dead, in dreams, visions and through other mystical experiences. One could also be summoned into the service by a deity during an ecstatic trance at a religious gathering.

Categorization of Medical Practitioners

Ekechukwu (cited in Madu, 2004), categorized medical practitioners in Africa into two:

1. The herbalist (*dibia ogwu*)
2. The diviner (*dibia afa*)

Mume (cited in Madu, 2004), further identifies eight types of medical practitioners:

1. The general practitioners
2. The herbalist (specializes in herbal application) and native doctors (inclined to supernatural powers)
3. Faith healers (here patients are forced to confess their sins, ones done they become emotionally healed)
4. Bone setters
5. The native gynaecologist and midwife
6. The witchdoctor who specializes in wizard-caused diseases, most of them being formally wizards and witches
7. The blood letter (the use of horn or other means to let bad blood out of the body)
8. Traditional surgeon

Not minding the further categorization made by Mume, they could still fall into Elechukwu's division of medical practitioners into *dibia afa* and *dibia ogwu*.

As already established, the medical practitioners in African traditional societies belong to a group of sacred specialists, and as members of the same group, it is not surprising that they would sometimes overlap in the performance of their functions. For instance, among the Ndebele, Hughes and Van (1954) observe that the medicine-man performs functions that belong to the priest and diviners. He combats witchcrafts by sending them back to their authors. There are times when he performs sacrifices on behalf of the sick; in this case he plays the role of a priest. When he tries to trace the cause of a sickness or misfortune, either as coming from spiritual world or human, he performs the work of a diviner. During burial, the medicine man does the ceremony of 'striking the grave', if the person has died of witchcraft. During this ceremony, the son or brother of the dead person visits the grave together with the medicine man. The medicine man carries the medicated stick and strikes the grave saying, "so and so, wake up! Go and fight". The spirit of the dead person leaves the grave and goes to fight the person who is believed to have killed him or her. Among the Azande, Mbiti (1969) observes that the medicine man sometimes performs the function of a prophet. He warns the people of impending danger. The overlap of the functions of sacred specialists could be explained from the fact that the African universe is interconnected.

Conclusion

Although modern life and Christianity is spreading in most African cities, traditional medical practitioners are still relevant to many Africans. Politicians who are afraid of opponents consult them, church authorities who want to overwhelm their congregations with miracles and thus keep them visit them, young men and women who are in love with other and who intend to preserve their love visit them for love portions, students at secondary and university levels visit them to help them pass their examinations, business men and women patronize them for success in business, etc. Daily, city dwellers match their ways into villages in search of them to help them solve their problems. And because of the high demand of their services in the cities, many medicine men and women are moving into the cities to provide services. From this, one gets the impression that medicine men will continue to be relevant, especially as they help to solve modern problems in a traditional way that seem to make more impact.

References

Ademuwagun, Z. (1979). *African therapeutic systems*. London: Waltham crossroad.

Arinze, F. (2008). *Sacrifice in Igbo religion*. Onitsha: St Stephen.

Evans-Pritchard, E. E. (1937). *Witchcraft, oracles and magic among the Azande* Oxford: Oxford University.

Egbeke, A. (2001). *Metaphysics: An introduction*. Enugu: Donze.

Ityavyar, D. A. (1982). Background to the development of health services in Nigeria. *Social Sciences and Medicine. 24*, 477- 490.

Ityavyar, D. A. (1984). Traditional and modern medicine: Possible patterns of integration. *Contact. 70*, 4-7.

Ityavyar, D. A. (1990)..African traditional medicine with reference to a wholistic view of sickness and health. In Metuh, E. and Olowo, O. (ed). *Nigerian Cultural Heritage* (pp. 233-247). Jos: Imico.

Hume, D. (1978). *A treatise on human nature*. Oxford: Oxford University.

Hammond-Took, W. D. (1960). *The Bantu speaking people of Southern Africa*. London: Rutledge and Kegan Paul.

Hughe,s A. J. B. & Van, V. J. (1954). *The Shona and Ndebele of Southern Rhodsia*. London: Burns and Oats.

Mbiti, J. (1969). *African religions and philosophy*. Nairobi: East African Educational.

Maclean, U. (1971). *Magical medicine*. London: Co and Whymath.

Madu, E. (2004). *Honest to African cultural heritage*. Imo: Franedoh.

Onuigbo, N. (2009). *The three worlds in Igbo traditional religion*. Enugu, Delta.

Quarcoopom, T. N. O. (1987). *West African traditional medicine*. Ibadan: African Universities.

Twumasi (1975). *Medical systems in Ghana: Studies in sociology of medicine*. Accra: Ghana.

Shakespeare, W. (1996). *The Twelfth Night*. In the complete works of William Shakespeare. Oxford: Shakespeare Head.

CHAPTER SIX

NATURE AND FUNCTION OF LOGIC IN AFRICAN EPISTEMOLOGY

Ejikemeuwa, J. O. Ndubisi, Ph.D.

Executive Summary

In philosophy, Western or African, logic and epistemology are very fundamental. They constitute the major branches of philosophy. They are concerned with the object and method of human knowledge. Remove knowledge, human life would be meaningless; any neglect on logic makes a particular claim to knowledge questionable and difficult for general acceptance. One thing to note is that without logic in epistemology, true or valid knowledge may not be attained. Every society has its own stock of epistemological thoughts, methods and world views. Since the quest for knowledge is part of human nature, there is no culture or tradition that is devoid of this essential quality. The African also has his own method or means of acquiring knowledge. The question now is: How logical are these African modes of acquiring knowledge? Put in another way: What is the role of logic in the African way of acquiring knowledge? The attempt to answer this question is the concern of this paper.

Keywords: Nature, Function, Logic, African, Epistemology

Introduction

Knowledge acquisition is central to the being of the human person. Every human person, whether young or old, desires to know. The quest for knowledge therefore is not the exclusive preserve of any group of people. It is something that characterizes our being human. In this regard Omoregbe as cited in Ozumba (2004:40) maintains that the human nature and experience are basically the same all over the world and that the tendency to philosophize is part of human nature. The implication of this assertion is that the capacity to acquire knowledge is innate in human beings.

Every human person, regardless of colour, race, status, location, etc., has the potentiality to acquire knowledge.

In philosophy, Western or African, logic and epistemology are very fundamental. They constitute the major branches of philosophy. They are concerned with the object and method of human knowledge. Remove knowledge, human life would be meaningless; any neglect on logic makes a particular claim to knowledge questionable and difficult for general acceptance. One thing to note is that without logic in epistemology, true or valid knowledge may not be attained. Ozumba (2004:40) observed that every society has its own stock of epistemological thoughts, methods and world views. Since the quest for knowledge is part of human nature, there is no culture or tradition that is devoid of this essential quality. The African also has his own method or means of acquiring knowledge. The question now is: How logical are these African modes of acquiring knowledge? Put in another way: What is the role of logic in the African way of acquiring knowledge? The attempt to answer this question is the concern of this paper. Therefore, this paper takes a look at the understanding of the concepts: logic and African epistemology, the modes of acquiring knowledge in African epistemology, the functions of logic in African epistemology. It later ends with a concluding reflection.

Logic: An Overview

The art of sound, correct and critical reasoning is in the domain of logic. Logic concerns itself with the proper method of reasoning. It distinguishes correct reasoning from incorrect reasoning; removes ambiguities and obscurities from human discourse. Logic brings out truth from falsity, consistency from inconsistency, orderliness from disorder, valid argument from invalid argument. Logic dissipates confusion that usually arises in our everyday discourse. It is logic that differentiates rational beings from irrational beings. The proper application of logic is what separates human beings from the lower animals.

In the view of Bello (2000:1), logic is concerned with the study of the principles and techniques of distinguishing good arguments from bad argument. The implication of Bello's position is that logic has to do with the proper structures of thinking. It provides the platform for coherent thinking. Copi (1982:2) emphatically states that logic studies the method and principles by which we differentiate good reasoning from bad reasoning and correct reasoning from incorrect reasoning. Aja (2008:3) observed thus:

> The basic aim of logic is to teach us to reason correctly. Reasoning is the activity or process of adducing, collecting reasons, weighing them, and drawing conclusions based upon these reasons. Correct reasoning is the art of finding reasons and/or evidence which do, in fact, support and/or prove our conclusion.

The observation of Aja presupposes that without logic, correct reasoning will be impossible. More so, for any claim to be acceptable, there must be some convincing evidence to support the claim, otherwise, it may not be regarded as true knowledge. This is because of the simple fact that it lacks convincing justification. Echekwube (1999) as cited in Jaja and Badey (2012:96) noted that "logic … is concerned with the processes of thinking and reasoning as well as the symbolic expressions of such process in verbal or written form." Logic also deals with the use of language for proper communication and comprehension. The inherent relationship between logic and language, in the view of Jaja and Badey, explains why logicians critically examine statements used in language to see if conclusions follow from the premise or premises (Jaja and Bradey, 2012:96). In sum, logic helps the individual to form arguments properly for better communication. It is logic that sharpens our thinking faculty and purifies the way we reason.

African Epistemology

The desire to know is innate in every human being. Every day, we make claim to certain knowledge. We even go as far as arguing for the thing that we claim to know. But some basic questions arise: What actually do we know? Is knowledge relative or objective? Can there be absolute claim to knowledge? What is the foundation for the knowledge we claim to have? The answers to the above questions form the subject matter of epistemology. Epistemology deals with the nature, origin and basis of human knowledge. Omoregbe (1998:vi) relates that epistemology as a major branch of philosophy is "the study of human knowledge, the study of the nature of human knowledge, its origin, its scope, its limits, its justification, its reliability or otherwise, its certainty or otherwise. It is like knowledge taking a critical look at itself to justify itself." In the view of Eboh (1998:1), epistemology simply deals with the justification of human knowledge. It examines the validity or truth of human knowledge (Eboh:1998:2). It is clear from the views of Omoregbe and Eboh that epistemology basically deals with justification of knowledge claim. So it is not enough for one to claim to know something; one has to show that what one claims to know is the case. For instance if I say that Ikechukwu Kanu is a Catholic priest or that Very Rev. Msgr. Prof. J. B. Akam is the Founder of Tansian University, I have to present evidence to substantiate or justify the claim. If not, such a claim is nonsense and therefore should not be regarded as knowledge.

> [A]ny claim to knowledge presupposes, if it is to be a valid claim, the satisfaction of conditions concerning grounds, truth, meaning and perhaps other things. To investigate these conditions is a philosophical task. To establish these general conditions is to elucidate the concept of knowledge, and this is a prime task of a philosopher concerned with the theory of knowledge [Epistemology]. (Hamlyn, 1977:5).

African epistemology is one of the major branches of African philosophy. We must note that African philosophy, in sum, has to do with a critical reflection on the African and the African world. Just like every other aspect of African philosophy, African epistemology has been observed to be in a bad state conceptually (Ozumba, 2004:35). The fact is that Africans have been regarded as those who do not reflect or reason but simply appeal to emotion. They are simply emotional beings rather than rational beings. It is against this misconception that Omoregbe (1985) as cited in Ozumba (2004:40) categorically stated that human nature and human experience are basically the same all over the world and the tendency to philosophize is part of human nature; all human beings reflect on some fundamental philosophic questions about life or about the universe. African epistemology therefore is the concretization of what is known in the African world. It is all about the way the African reflects on the reality within the African world. It also has to do with the ways and manners the African makes effort to justify what he claims to know. Aja in Uduigwomen (2002:36) pointed out that the problem of knowledge in traditional African thought is that of ascertaining whether or not what is claimed as knowledge is actually knowledge rather than mistaken opinion on the other hand, and the means or source of acquiring the knowledge on the other. In the view of Ozumba (2001:171), African epistemology has to do with Africa's own way of carrying out its enquiries into the nature, scope and limits of knowledge. Now the pertinent question is: What is that Africa's own way of knowledge acquisition? It is simply the mode or manner through which the African talks about reality in the African world. It must be observed that there are varied ways and means of knowledge acquisition in Africa. Let us now look at the forms of knowledge acquisition in African epistemology.

Forms of Knowledge in African Epistemology:

There are varied forms of knowledge in African epistemology. They include: perceptual knowledge, common sense knowledge, old age knowledge, inferential knowledge, mystical knowledge, oral tradition, wholistic knowledge, etc. Let us briefly analyze them to enable us have a better understanding of the ways and manners of knowledge acquisition in African epistemology.

1. **Perceptual Knowledge:**

As the name implies, this type of knowledge is gained through sense perception. It is called first-hand knowledge. The African person holds that knowledge is gained through what we see, hear, touch, taste or smell. This is embedded on the idea of Igbo expression: 'afu n'anya e kwere' (to see is to believe). The idea that 'Mr. John is in the class' or that 'Snow is falling now' is within the domain of perceptual knowledge. The African finds it very difficult to doubt what he has witnessed with the empirical senses. The question of whether one is deceived by his senses is out of place here. In some cases where there are problems of ascertaining the veracity of claim to knowledge, the African would ask for the eye-witness (the third party). But should the testimony of the eye-witness be doubted, oath-taking becomes the final reference point.

2. **Common Sense Knowledge:**

This is the type of knowledge that is gained effortlessly. It is the type of knowledge that is coeval with the human person. It is believed that every human person has this type of knowledge: the knowledge to distinguish between what is morally good or morally bad. It must be noted that the fact that every person possesses this type of knowledge is in kind and not in degree. The Igbo people would always say that 'Isi na isi ha bu n'onu' (That all heads are equal is just a matter of words of mouth). The implication here is that some people's common sense knowledge may be higher than others.

3. **Old Age Knowledge:**

This is the type of knowledge gained through wealth of experience. The Africans believe that the older a person is the more knowledgeable he/she becomes. It is also believed that the old person must have had series of experience in life which will now be the basis for most of his decisions. Also, in the African hierarchy of beings, there is the belief that the old people are closer to the gods who are the sources of all wisdom. So the ontological states of old people within the African world presuppose knowledgeability. A person is said to know or have wisdom in as much as he approaches divine wisdom. And a person approaches divine wisdom when he/she becomes less fleshy (Onyewuenyi, 1980:312). This simply means that the older a person gets, the more knowledgeable he is.

4. **Inferential Knowledge:**

Simply put, inference is the act of drawing conclusion from a given fact or data. So inferential knowledge is the type of knowledge gained from repeated events or phenomena. If a little child says the truth once, twice or trice, the African elder concludes that the little child is truthful. This type of knowledge / conclusion is amplified by the past experiences. However, there is a problem that goes with this form of knowledge which is not within the scope of this study. The important thing to note is that the African in his quest for knowledge tries to make reference to the past to enable him ascertain the present.

5. **Mystical Knowledge:**

This is the type of knowledge acquired through extra-ordinary means. It is beyond the ordinary sense perception. It is the type of knowledge gained through the help of the God, deities and other spiritual beings. It is a form of knowledge that is the exclusive preserve of some individuals. The African believes that those who are privileged to possess this type of knowledge are the diviners, priests, native-doctors, witches, rain-makers, etc. Uduigwomen (2002:38) observed that these set of people are believed to possess certain "innate abilities" that enable them to manipulate the spirit world in favour of the natural world. Ekarika (1984) argued that this type of knowledge has to do with obtaining information or truth about the past and the future things. Umontong (2002:34) also noted that among the Annang people of Nigeria, mystical knowledge is the major determinant of truth that is beyond ordinary man's understanding. One thing to note about this type of knowledge is that it is African's own way of gaining knowledge of realities that are ordinarily hidden.

6. **Oral Tradition:**

This is the form of knowledge gained through words of mouth. It is the major means of knowledge acquisition and transmission in the African traditional society. Oral tradition has to do with the accumulation of events handed down from one generation to the other in form of proverb, myths, stories, folk-tales, customs, legends, etc. Some of the things we claim to know today are the things handed down to us through oral tradition. This form of knowledge acquisition is very important to the African person. More so, this form of knowledge disposes the African child to be in tune with the demands of his immediate society. Uduigwomen cited Ajayi's position on oral tradition as a source of knowledge in African epistemology. He noted that oral tradition is sometimes enshrined in the works of arts, crafts, symbols, titles, names of places, shrines and sacred places (Uduigwomen, 2002:39).

7. **Wholistic Knowledge:**

It is the belief of the African person that knowledge of reality cannot be gained if the individual person detaches himself from it. This implies that knowledge of a given reality must involve the subject and the object, the knower and the known. This is what is known as wholistic knowledge in African epistemology. Anyanwu and Ruch (1981:94) declared thus: "The African maintained that there can be no knowledge of reality if an individual detaches himself from it." It therefore follow that there is a connection or a relationship that exists between the African person and his world. The African does not claim to know anything in isolation.

Having stated the forms of knowledge in African epistemology, we shall now look at the functions of logic in African epistemology.

Functions of Logic in African Epistemology

Logic, as noted earlier, has to do with the structure of thinking. Every culture has its own peculiar way of reasoning. This is the sense in which we talk of African logic. Momoh (1989:174) writes:

> In everyday usage of natural language we talk of a person as being logical if he is reasonable, sensible and intelligent; if he can unemotionally and critically evaluate evidence or a situation; if he can avoid contradictions, inconsistency and incoherence, or if he can hold a point of view argue for and from it, summon counter-examples and answer objections.

It is the view of Momoh as cited above that there are people who are logical in the sense stated above. Consequently, Africa is not an exception. Logic in African epistemology deals with the application of reason to the world and culture of the African, to his language and objects of his reference (Jaja & Badey, 2012:97). For instance, when a bird cries at night and a person dies in the morning, the African elders conclude that the cry of the bird at night is the cause of the death in the morning. This type of conclusion was not reached after single occurrence; it was based on several cases of witnessing a particular bird crying at night and a person dying in the morning. The simple fact that the African did not just arrive at a conclusion after a single occurrence goes to show the logicality or rationality of the African person. However, our concern here is not on African logic per se, but on the functions of logic in knowledge acquisition in African epistemology.

The function of logic in knowledge acquisition is quite enormous. Without logic the study of African epistemology will be greatly impaired. There is this Igbo adage: "Ilu bu mmanu ndi Igbo ji eri okwu" (Proverb is the oil Igbo people use in 'eating' words). Put differently, we can say that logic is the key with which we can use to unlock knowledge. The implication of this statement is that logic is very essential in epistemology whether African or Western. A person may claim to know something, but without the tools of logic, he may not be able to present his ideas very well. And when ideas are not properly presented, the particular claim to knowledge is inhibited. In a general sense, we can say that logic purifies our thinking pattern and makes us critical in our reasoning. More so, we affirm that without the application of logic in epistemology, true and certain knowledge may be very difficult if not impossible to attain. Let us now highlight some of the functions of logic in African epistemology:

1. Avoidance of Error:

Error simply means a departure from what is proper. It is an act of giving assent to a false claim. It also means a movement away from the truth. The study of logic therefore helps the African to stick to true knowledge and avoid accepting any knowledge that is erroneous. This can be ascertained by following the rules of logic. In African epistemology, logic guards the African against the habit of drawing conclusions from premises that are totally unrelated to the stated conclusion. This is one of the ways by which logic makes knowledge acquisition to be free from error.

2. Correct / Sound Reasoning:

Logic provides the African with the necessary tools to engage in correct and sound reasoning. It makes it possible for African epistemologist to be able to evaluate arguments in order to distinguish the correct one from the incorrect. The study of logic improves the reasoning capacity of the African person. Thus we can say that logic sharpens the thinking faculty of the African. The African person is not only an emotional being as argued in some quarters, but more so, a rational being. This is exemplified in his quest for evidence for any knowledge claim.

3. Clarity of Expression:

Some claims to knowledge are sometimes too blurred and confusing. Also, some ideas and expressions are often packaged in obscurity. A person may claim to know something but the illogical presentation can downplay his claim to knowledge, thereby creating confusion and making it very difficult for people to comprehend what is being said. It is the function of logic to sift out clarity in knowledge acquisition. Logic therefore provides African epistemology with the systematic and coherent ways of acquiring and expressing knowledge.

4. Prediction of Event / Decision-Making:

Another important function of logic in African epistemology is that it facilitates the act of prediction of events. With the help of logic, the African person, most especially the elderly, can predict events with a high level of accuracy. This is based on past experience. Logic enables the African to reason critically before taking decisions especially when faced with difficulties.

5. The Power of Persuasion:

Logic provides the African epistemologists with the necessary tools to be able to distinguish between persuasion based on certain psychological techniques and the one based on rational argument and supporting evidence.

6. Avoidance of Fallacy:

A fallacy is an argument whose conclusion is not derived from the premises given. Aja (2008:115) states that in logic "fallacious argument is one in which the premises, even if true, would never entail nor justify the premises that is drawn." With the study of logic, the African gets to know and learn the varied classes of fallacies. This provides the African with the ample opportunity to detect easily any violation of logical principle.

Concluding

So far, this paper has concerned itself with the analysis of the nature and functions of logic in African epistemology. It emphasized that the African can possess no knowledge if the individual detaches himself from the world. This implies that knowledge acquisition in African epistemology is a combination / co-operation of all his faculties. His senses, imagination and reason are involved in the process of acquiring knowledge. It is through this way that the African can claim to have acquired knowledge. We therefore note that the general method by which the African arrives at a reliable knowledge of reality is through personal experience guided by logic. Logic plays a vital role in knowledge acquisition in African epistemology.

Going through this work, one will discover that logic is a *conditio sine qua non* for knowledge acquisition. Without logic the African person may not be balanced in his quest for knowledge. Therefore, we affirm that logic provides African epistemologist with the necessary tools to separate real knowledge from illusion; to sift correct reasoning from incorrect reasoning. The study of logic makes the African to be systematic, coherent and critical in his reasoning. Logic therefore provides the ground / foundation for accepting any claim to knowledge. It disposes the African epistemologist to ask for evidence before accepting any claim to knowledge. One important point to note is that the function of logic in African epistemology has to be viewed through the focal lens of the African person as a being in the African world.

References

Aja, E., *Logic and Clear Thought: An Invitation to good reasoning 2nd ed.*, (Enugu: University of Nigeria Press, 2008).

Anyanwu, K. C. & Ruch, E. A., *African Philosophy: An Introduction to the Main Philosophical Trends in Contemporary Africa* (Rome: Catholic Book Agency – Officium Libri Catholic, 1981).

Bello, A. *Introduction to Logic* (Ibadan: University Press, 2000).

Copi, I. M, *Introduction to Symbolic Logic* (New York: Macmillan, 1982).

Eboh, B. O., *Basic Issues in the Theory of Knowledge* (Nsukka: Fulladu Publishing Company, 1995).

Ekarika, J. P., *From Nature to Divine: An Introduction to the Study of Religions* (Italy: 1984).

Hamlyn, D. W., *The Theory of Knowledge,* (London: The MacMillan Press Ltd., 1977).

Jaja, J. M. & Badey, P.P., "Logic in African Philosophy: Examples from two Niger Delta Societies" *International Journal of Academic Research in Business and Social Sciences, vol. 2. No. 4* (2012), Pp. 95 – 102.

Momoh, C. S. (ed.), *The Substance of African Philosophy* (Auchi: African Philosophy Projects Publications, 1989).

Omoregbe, J., *Epistemology: A Systematic and Historical Study* (Lagos: Joja Educational Research & Publications Ltd., 1998).

Onyewuenyi, I., "Is There An African Philosophy?" in Claude Summer (ed.) *African Philosophy,* (Addis Ababa: Addis Ababa University Press, 1980).

Ozumba, G. O. *A Concise Introduction to Epistemology* (Calabar: Ebeneger Printing Press, 2001).

Ozumba, G. O., *A Colloquium on African Philosophy, vol. 2* (Enugu: University of Nigeria Press, 2004).

Uduigwomen, A. F. (ed.), *Footmarks on African Philosophy,* (Lagos: Obaroh and Ogbinaka Publishers Ltd., 2002).

Umontong, I. D., "Truth: A Philosophical Reflection on Africa", *Sophia: African Journal of Philosophy, vol 2. No. 2 (2002), pp 25 – 39.*

CHAPTER SEVEN

PRACTICING PARTICIPATORY DEMOCRACY IN NIGERIA

Paul T. Haaga Ph.D.

Executive Summary

Many people believe that democracy which is the "rule of the majority" is an indispensable form of government. This explains why democracy has become the most fashionable form of governance in the world. In most societies of the world today, the issue is not which political system is appropriate but rather when will the society become democratized or fully democratic. A strong and effective democratic process should be able to establish a functioning administrative structure, and address the issue of how leaders are chosen and how they should act for the interest of the people they are representing. This paper points out some major methodological problems by addressing the case of egalitarianism in the Nigerian democratic structure. It also illustrates the nexus between freedom and democracy. The paper suggests participatory democracy, enhanced by the use of information and communication technology as a way to meaningful development in Africa.

Keywords: Governance, Nigeria, Participatory, Democracy

Introduction

The practice of democracy in Africa presents the immediate problem of defining democracy as a concept, and then deciding if Western definitions even holds-water in Africa. The fact is that democratic social organization is the best culture for ensuring the fullest development and expression of each person's unique talents and life purposes; genuine democracy involves far more than periodic voting for politicians it requires intelligent, active participation in the formation of values that regulate the living of men people together. On this note, Dewey (1974) insists that all those who are affected by social institutions must have a share in producing and managing them.

Participatory democracy through active citizen participation enhances the quality of decisions, policies and laws thus contributing to the amelioration of the quality of life of citizens. People must be able to contribute to how they are governed; they must be able to ask questions and intervene in the procedure. The crucial questions regarding democracy in Africa are: is Africa underdeveloped because it is primarily undemocratic? Or is Africa undemocratic because it is primarily underdeveloped? Which is cause and which is effect? In responding to these questions, this paper examines the tenants of democracy in Nigeria; it outlines the challenges of the democracy practiced in Nigeria and finally suggests participatory democracy which involves change, reorientation, personal responsibility and active participation as the way to meaningful development in Africa.

On the Conceptand Values ofDemocracy: A comment from Plato

Democracy is etymologically derived from two Greek words, *Demos* meaning 'people' and *kratein* meaning 'to rule'. It means rule of the people. Abraham Lincoln classically defined it as "government of the people, by the people and for the people". Strictly speaking, government by all the people should mean unanimous decisions in the welfare of the people (Sabine and Thorson, 1973). But this of course, is impossible in political matters. Lincoln's addition of "government for the people", in Rousseau's *Theory of the General will*, means the decisive view, which invariably must be that of the majority and should seek to serve the interest of all, even though it does not have the agreement of all (Raphael, 1976).Aristotle defines democracy as "the rule of many for the good of the poor" as opposed to oligarchy, which asserts "the rule of the few for the good of the wealthy". Aristotle makes this contrast to indicate the intrinsic character of the two polities: whereas in oligarchy, the rulers are few because there are only few people who are wealthy, in democracy there are many because liberty is enjoyed by all alike (Aristotle, 1981: III, v. 7). Democracy means "a system of government where people organize and realize their wishes through the instrument of the law they have made for themselves" (Njoku, 2002). The assumed relationship between participatory democratically elected leaders and the citizens is based on reciprocity. As such the people make the laws themselves and the binding force of this law can only be realized when the people participate actually in the making of these laws, rather than in just delegating people to do this on their behalf.

It is not the questions of how many political parties exist or partake in government but most essentially how they, together with other public institutions function and how are the basic democratic values demonstrated?   These values (of democracy include) freedom, equality, justice, self-responsibility, accountability, openness and transparency in government; and these values distinguish democracy from other political ideas and forms of government. Plato describes the ends of democracy as freedom, equality and variety(Horowitz, 2003). But he criticizes democracy precisely because these loading features namely, freedom, equality, justice, self-responsibility, openness and transparency are not always obtainable. Freedom in the sense of "doing what you like" is attractive but it cannot last, and it is further less desirable than doing the right thing. Plato further opines that, equality is wrong because it goes against nature; men are unequal in their capacities and should be given different functions in accordance with their different capacities (Plato, 1987).

Democracy and Good Governance: the Africa Experience

African democracy originated in "chiefless societies", and democracy reached its highest development where the people actually governed themselves without chiefs, where self-government was a way of life, and "law and order" were taken for granted. The lineage ties and responsibilities and the age-grade or age-set system were the earliest institutions through the African constitution functioned, and out of which its democracy was born (Wiliams, 1987). After a while, democracy in Africa became an experimental process in a new generation of countries. Truly democratic participation is self-motivated and self-determined; it is not coerced. Currently In Africa, democracy implies a commitment to the self-motivated assertion of some few individuals with egoistic interests in political affairs.There is a massive a campaign for one particular system of government, commonly known as democracy, which is presented by many as the only valid system of government for all peoples in all places and circumstances.

In Africa, different forms of government were tried out by different peoples at different stages of their history. Before colonial rule was imposed on the nations of Africa, it was impossible to invent a common name for the different forms of government that existed among its various peoples (Onah, 2004). Also, it is pertinent to note that in the recent past, Africa witnessed political liberations from authoritarian regimes to democratic systems. The liberation has mostly culminated into multiparty democracies. Multi-party politics has been perceived and pursued as end itself rather than as means to the fundamental goals of human satisfaction, happiness and dignity. To buttress this point, Chidam'modzi opines that "it has also been apparent that democracy has been construed as merely multipartiyism" (2004).

Notwithstanding, people may disagree about the best means of achieving good governance, but they quite agree that good governance is absolutely imperative for social and economic progress (Oburota, 2003).What is governance and what makes governance good or bad? This is perhaps a philosophical question which may attract endless and multifarious answers. Fundamentally, the question of good and bad is ethical/moral. According to Madhav (2007) good governance has much to do with the ethical grounding of governance and must be evaluated with reference to specific norms and objectives as may be laid down.

In most societies of the world today, the issue is not which political system is appropriate but rather when will the society become democratized or fully democratic. The democratization project is therefore regarded as the age of advancement that every society should strive to attain (Owolabi, 2001). Democracy has thus been recognized as the only moral and legitimate way through which a society can be administered (Oluwole, 2004). Indeed, effective democratic forms of governance rely on public participation, accountability and transparency. In this regard, democracy not only prescribes how political power should be acquired but also what to do with it or how it should be exercised. Therefore, democracy specifies who constitutes the legitimate government and wields the authority inherent in the state, how they acquire authority and how they are to exercise it (Parekh, 1993). This makes democracy amenable to moral and ethical justifications or judgments. Hence, good governance forms the philosophical foundation upon which democracy and democratic theories are built.

But then one wonders if Nigeria is practicing a conventional democratic system of government or a democratic system of government peculiar to Nigeria alone? In regard to this, Nwigwe (2004) observes that it would constitute a very difficult problem for political theorist to determine the classification of Nigeria's type of governments. It is not a monarchy, even though there are so many monarchs in the policy making positions. It is definitely not an aristocracy, because by its very definition, aristocracy means government by the best. It is of course not democracy because at least in its modern understanding, democracy is government of the people by the people and for the people. What then is it? The fact is, Nigerians has not significantly reaped the dividends of democracy, because the strength of democracy lies in its concept of all-inclusiveness which is registered in the phrase: government for the majority. Let us see the misconception of democracy in Africa.

Nigeria and the Question of Democracy

The history of Nigeria's democracy is a history of duplicity and fraud. Largely supervised by a cabal within the military, our so called 'transition to democracy'was actually transitions to feudalism and Autocracy more often than not leading to the ends. These transitions were not tailored to lead the nation into democracy because the architects were often concerned more with their personal, class or regional interests rather than those of the nation (Kukah, 2009). The saddest aspect of Nigeria's democracy has been the absence of a coherent programme of transition dedicated to ending authoritarianism and immunity, leading to genuine democracy. The Nigerian problem is the unwillingness or inability of its leaders to rise to the responsibility, to the challenge of personal example which are the hallmarks of true leadership (Achebe, 1983).

In an ideal democratic system, the people are supposed to be the ones through their elected representatives,to make decisions that would be binding on all. It is rather unfortunate that the so-called democracy practiced in Nigeria is pluralistic dictatorships in which selfish and unscrupulous tyrant ride on their subjects in order to defend their personal interests. Little wonder Onah (2004) redefined the Nigerian democracy as government of the people, by the parties, for the powerful; or as exploitation of the people, by the powerful, through the parties. With some of these imbedded features in the Nigerian democracy, one will conclude thatNigerian politicians see democracy in instrumental terms and are not committed to democracy as an end and concur with those who are of the opinion that "only a tiny handful of people make decisions that shape the lives of all of us despite the elaborate rituals of parties, elections and interest group actively, we have little direct influence over these decisions" (Dye and Zeigler, 2000).

The task of combining democracy and development in Nigeria seems harder especially with the era of globalization, and the abuses of human and civil rights; equality and freedom are major pillars of democracy but how pragmatic is this in the Nigerian democracy, a system where most office holders or politicians have immunity from prosecution while in office. Commenting on freedom, Baah, (2000) states, "the focus on individual as a free being is western and really difficult to apply to African", collective rights take precedence over social and economic rights, which in turn precede over civil and political rights. Freedom of expression of the press is fundamental to democracy, but even with the bill passed on the 'freedomofinformation'; to what extent can we say the press is free? This is only an illusion which is dubious and deceptive. What we have today is a politicized press and it is hijacked by the so-called powerful or influential people in the society. How can there be a meaningful development in such a deceptive democratic system? It is on this regard, that this piece adopts a revolutionary dimension by proposing participatory democracy as a way to meaningful development to Africa. Revolution in this sense means, change which takes place within a short period geared towards restructuring of power or organizational structures and it is more obtainable in a democratic system of government where the operative systems are stagnant and redundant.

The relevance of Information in Participatory Democracy

The ideological orientation of the move to participatory democracy consists in the dropping of egotism and the picking of altruism. Participating in a democracy by voting is one part of a larger freedom that allows the citizens of a community, and our nation, to make change. A free press is one part of a larger freedom because it gives citizens the right to be informed, this not just altruism but also a culture of information, for the inflow and outflow of information is one of the fundamental values of participatory democracy (Brown, 2011). This freedom of information is so fundamental to participatory democracy, because in order to make fruitful and useful contribution to policy formulation in Africa, individuals must be informed. And the limitation of vital information about policy and governance to just a small share of those in governance, restricts democracy to representation rather than participation. As such, the flow of information is vital for there to be participation. The freedom of information despite the information bill past in Nigeria, still is in doubt. This quest for information informs his question that, how can we build an era where information will be more important than money? The fact here is that free flows of information enhances and have great influence on any democratic system (Theobald, 2004).

It is this quest for genuine communication rather than domination that informs Habermas' (1997) discourse in his *The Theory of communicative Action*, where he makes the case that, the life world has been colonized by system and that media is what makes this process possible. It does this because of its ability to help individual's co-ordinate their actions on large scale whole pursuing individual interest at an instrumental level towards the world. That media stride interaction is an alternative to communicative understanding, thus the emphasis should be on expression rather than attempts to impress intellectual pride and linguistic pedantry. The point we are driving at here is that one ideological backdrop for participatory democracy is the fact of co-ordinate communication of all based on information from all and for all.

Technology has a role to play, in this regard and this takes off from Theobald's projection that our new capacity to gather, store and reproduce information signals a motion to information. But it is obvious that this capacity has been used wrongly, as such instead of technology helping to liberate man, it has only helped in dominating man. Since a new model for man is required for this level of democratic re-orientation, we are making a case for a new model of technology that will also be vital at this point. Technology here is at the service of man not man at the service of technology. Regarding technology, Jungk (1997) writes, "this revitalization of democracy could be assisted by electronic communications techniques, which can bring distant objects close and unite partners in discussion however for apart they may be". Technically, this can be described as the role of cyber space technology on participatory democracy.

The best example in this regard is what president Barrack Obama did sometime in the "High Tech town Hall" in United State. Therewere avenues created via the web where the president himself was available in person to entertain questions from the public with regard to policy issues. For those without direct access to the venue because of space, could use the internet. It was also far reaching because the internet is also at every corner of the United State. But in the case of Nigeria where the internet services are restricted to some places, we could use the television or radio station, by so doing; we shall see the use of cyberspace technology for more involvement of the people in policy making, and for clarification of some policy formulations.

On the possibilities of practicing Participatory Democracy in Africa (Nigeria)

The fundamental goals of participatory democracy are: (a) making the leaders accountable and answerable for their actions and policies; (b) making the citizens effective participants in choosing their leaders and regulating their actions; (c) making the society as open, and the economy as transparent as possible; and (d) making the social order just and equitable to the greatest number possible. To this, we observe that given the right conditions and factors, participatory democracy provides a solid foundation for good governance which is essential for nation building (Mukherjee and Ramaswamy, 2012).

Participatory democracy is a process emphasizing the broad participationof constituents in the direction and operation of political systems; it is a call for people's participation in actual governance rather than being relegated just to the point of voting. However, it tends to advocate more involved forms of citizen participation than traditional representative democracy. Participatory democracy strives to create opportunities for all members of a political group to make meaningful contributions to decision-making, and seeks to broaden the range of people who have access to such opportunities. It adopts elements of direct democracy and representative democracy and emphasizes the broad participation of constituents in the direction and operation of political systems. Though etymologically, democracy will mean participation, traditional representative democracies tend to limit citizens' participation to voting, leaving actual governance to politicians (Mukherjee and Ramaswamy, 2012). In order to experience full participatory democracy in

Nigeria, there must be participatory arrangements, which need to be open at their foundation to everyone affected by such decisions; the need for mutually agreed and openly negotiated rules to be upheld by everybody, and mechanisms for sanctioning deviants; an enabling environment for participatory institutions and groups to monitor implementation of government's decisions; and a general sharing of knowledge. What is most important is what eventually brings about good democratic practices that promote good governance to facilitate sustainable development in different settings (Babangida 2008).

In principle, democracy obviously requires both the existence of a civil society and respect for human rights. In reality, however, it is often seen merely in terms of the organization of elections. The degree of success of the system should be measured with reference to how far all the actors in society are actually involved; and this can be visible through the adoption of participatory democracy (Mukherjee and Ramaswamy, 2012). One quality which has always been lacking in Nigeria's political system in the past and present is people's participation in democracy. Even when democracy is in place, people are often pushed aside by the political forces at play. Power brokers do not often see the wisdom in involving the people in the crucial decisions taken to transform the society. The result of this negligence has been a massive failure of the system.

The basic idea of participatory democracy is that people need a new way to be involved in a broadened approach to local decision making. Participatory democracy has come to mean the right of citizens in a democracy to participate. It means the obligation of citizens to participate in the decisions made by their governmental representatives that impact the lives of all citizens (Brown, 2010). Surveys have shown that citizens no longer feel ownership of decisions which impact their lives. There is little or no trust between citizensand their elected officials in Nigeria. Every community is being overwhelmed with change which is transforming institutions. Too many people feel that they have to make sure that they get their fair share because of competition and lack of ethics. All of this leads to a society whose local communities no longer have a sense that the "common good" is possible. It is on this note that Jungk (1977) writes on this task that the quest for a man in this millennium, is, how the democracy of acclamation can be transformed into a democracy of participation. The people must wake up to reality and begin to ask their politicians questions such as, why do you want my vote? And he must treatthe easy answer of the politician with appropriate skepticism (Achebe, 1983).

Democracy as it were in Nigeria, only performs the duty of acclamation and needs to take up the role of participation. A great reversal of values will be pertinent and there will have to be a shift from isolation to openness, from conquest to expansion, from producing to experiencing, from forced achievement to free development, from hard to soft value system, from rigid to flexible way of life, from use to playful, from death –dealing to life giving. As such is this re-orientation of values for a more humanized democracy?We begin to see the truth of Yankelovich(2005) about the sudden up-surge of the right for self-expression.His general orientation is that: The spiritual and cultural development of the individual can only be accomplished within the solidarity of a community that has renounced egoistical surges such as careerism, the pursuit of profit, and consumer greed. It is through participatory democracy that a meaningful development can be attained on the ground were the people represented acknowledges and are aware of what is done on their behalf.

Conclusion

It is only through active participation in democracy that we can find a solid ground for meaningful and sustainable development in Nigeria, rather than mere representation. As it were, this piece advocate for political transparency, accountability and equity amongst Nigerian leaders, especially now where the maxim is "survival of the fittest". Participatory democracy brings to the fore the publicness of the public sphere, in this regard too Habermas (2007) even goes as far as stipulating guidelines for this form of discourse. Thus, in his essay "Discourse Ethics: Notes on a programme of philosophical justification", Habermas makes the case that the validity of moral norms cannot be justified in the mind of an isolated individual reflecting on the world. That this can only be ascertained inter subjectively. The proposal of participatory democracy also answers the question of the publicness of public opinion, for when avenues are created for public participation in opinion formation, and thenwe can truly talk about the public nature of public opinion. The basis for universality here is not just the logical structure of the positions nor their ontological composition or constitution, but the depth and the breadth of the participation is what matters.

References

Achebe, C., (1983). *The Trouble with Nigeria*, Enugu: Fourth Dimension Publication

Baah, R. A., (2006). *Human Rights in Africa: The Conflict of Implementation*, Lanham, MD: University Press of America.

Babangida, A.M., (2008). 'Participation is a key Element in a Democracy. Igbinedion University, Okada, Edo State, retrieved at http://sunday.dailytrust.com/index.php?option=com content&view=article&id=6651&catid=45&Itemid=109

Brown J., (2010). What is participatory democracy? Online retrieved at http://en.wikipedia.org/wiki/Participatory_democracy on 27th September, 2011

Chancellor Wiliams (1987). *The Destruction of Black Civilization*, Chicago: Third World press.

Chidam'modzi, H. F, (2004). "The problem of representation: dilemmas of African democracy" in Oguejiofor J Obi (Ed.) *Philosophy, Democracy and Responsible Governance in Africa*, Enugu: Delta Publication (Nigeria) Ltd

Dewey, J., (1975). "Democracy and Educational Administration," in Joseph Ratner, (Ed.), *Intelligence in the Modern World: John Dewey's Philosophy*. New York: Modern Library.

Dye, R. and Ziegler, H., (2000). *The Irony of Democracy*, Millenial edition, Harcour, Cambridge: Cambridge University Press.

Habermas J., (2007). *A Theory of Communicative Action: The Critique of Functionalist Reason*,trans by Thomas Mcarthy, Vol. 2 Cambridge: Polity Press.

Horowitz, D. (1993). "Democracy in Divided Societies," *Journal of Democracy*, no. 4, Vol. 4.

Jungk R., (1976). *The Everyman Project: Resources For A Humane Future*, London: Thomas and Hudson Limited.

Kukah, M, H, (2009). "Ten Years of Democracy in Nigeria" in Chiegboka A.B.C et al (Ed) in *The Humanities and Nigeria' Democratic Experience*, Awka: Rex Charles and Patrick Ltd.

Kukah, M. H., (1999). *Democracy And Civil Society in Nigeria*, Ibadan: Spectrum Books Limited

Madhav, G., (2007). Report of the one man Committee on Good Governance, July Human Right Watch (2007) "Election or "Selection"? Human Rights Abuse and Threats to Free and Fair Elections in Nigeria" online retrieved at http://hrw.org/backgrounder/africa/nigeria0407/index.ht.

Mukherjee S. and Ramaswamy, (2012). *A History of Political Thought Plato to Marx*, 2nded. New Delhi: PHI Private Limited.

Njoku, F.O.C., (2002). *Philosophy in Politics, Law and Democracy,*Owerri: Claretian Institute of Philosophy.

Nwigwe B. E., (2003). "Origin and Limits of State Authority" in Oguejiofor J Obi (Ed.) Philosophy, *Democracy and Responsible Governance in Africa*, Enugu: Delta Publication (Nigeria) Ltd.

Oburota, A., (2003). "Governance as a Source of Social Violence in Africa" in Oguejiofor J Obi (Ed.) *Philosophy, Democracy and Responsible Governance in Africa*, Enugu: Delta Publication (Nigeria) Ltd.

Oluwole SB., (2003). "Democracy and Indigenous Governance: The Nigerian Experience", in Oguejiofor J Obi (Ed.) *Philosophy, Democracy and Responsible Governance in Africa*, Enugu: Delta Publication (Nigeria) Ltd.

OnahI. G., (2004). "Africa and the Illusion of democracy" inOguejiofor J Obi (Ed.) *Philosophy, Democracy and Responsible Governance in Africa*, Enugu: Delta Publication (Nigeria) Ltd.

Owolabi K.A., (2003). "Can the Past Salvage the Future? Indigenous Democracy and the Quest for Sustainable Democratic Governance in Africa" in Oguejiofor J Obi (Ed.) *Philosophy, Democracy and Responsible Governance in Africa*, Enugu: Delta Publication (Nigeria) Ltd.

Parekh, B., (1993). "The Cultural Particularity of Liberal Democracy", in David Held (ed.) *Prospects for Democracy: North, South, East, West*, Chicago: Polity Press.

Participatory Democracy on line retrieved on 20th August, 2011 at http://en.wikipedia.org/wiki/Participatory_democracy

Raphael, D. D., (1976). *Problems of Political Philosophy*, London: Macmillan Press Ltd.

Raz, J, (2007).*Value, RespectandAttachment*, Cambridge: Cambridge Press.

Sabine, G. H. and Thorson T. L., *A History of Political Theory*, 4th ed., Oxford: IBH Publishing company.

Plato, (1987).*The Republic* trans by Desmond Lee, 2nd edition, New York: Pengiun Books, Book II, 357a–368c.

Yankelovic, D., (1974). *New Morality: A Profile of American Youth in the 70s*, New York.

CHAPTER EIGHT

POLITICAL GLOBALISM AND ITS IMPACT ON AFRICAN NATIONS

Onebunne, Jude Ifeanyichukwu PhD & Ufearoh, Anthony PhD

Executive Summary

Political globalism is a concept that affects all nations of the world. For centuries, globalization has progressively knitted together the world and created unity out of great diversity. Political globalism can be said to be the integration of different countries of the world into one political global order which is meant to benefit members of the entire society but, political globalism has not gone down well for most African countries especially developing African countries, as it has disintegrated what they used to have. This research therefore gives a clear meaning of political globalism in Africa, enunciates its importance and otherwise and discusses its effect on African political growth using the critical analysis method. This research work will also make possible suggestions on how Africans can manage political globalism such that will not be detrimental to African, culture, values, integration, unity, growth and development.

Keywords: Globalism, Africa, Politics, Growth, Development

Introduction

Globalism is a vast concept that cuts across all aspects of human existence. It is not restricted to a particular country but affects the entire world either positively or negatively. For centuries, globalization has progressively knitted together the world and created unity out of great diversity. According to Brittan (1998), globalisation is viewed "as a whirlwind of relentless and disruptive change which leaves governments helpless and leaves a trail of economic, social, cultural and environmental problems in its wake."(p. 2).

From obscure origins in French and American writings in the 1960s, the concept of globalization finds expression today in all of the worlds' major languages. Yet, it lacks precise definition. Indeed, globalization is in danger of becoming the cliché of our times (David, McGrew, Goldblatt & Perraton, 1999, p. 1).The phenomenon of globalization has indeed captured the centre stage of international relations in the post cold war world. Indeed, globalization mirrors cooperative as well as conflicting trends across states and civil societies between multiple ranges of actors, at varying levels, which shape contours of international relations. Understanding the trajectories of interactions between these multiple actors including nation states, international/ regional organizations, transnational firms and banks, multinational terrorist organizations and international social movements etc; under globalization, is incontestably, a daunting task. For, perceptions and perspectives on the complex themes underlying globalization tend to vary according to diverse schools of thought in international relations as well as the spatial locations of scholars (Harshe, 2004, p. 9). Since the last decade, globalization in its accelerated form has been setting the pace as well as the logic of international relations. Nevertheless, being a constantly evolving and an ongoing process, the term "globalization", continues to escape definition clarity. Broadly, however, it is deployed to describe an ongoing movement towards conceiving the world as a single unit and building the consciousness of the people towards the world as a whole (Sadeeque et al 2015 citing Robertson, 1992 as cited in Harshe, op.cit, p. 15).

Intriligator (2003) posits that globalization is a powerful real aspect of the new world system, and it represents one of the most influential forces in determining the future course of the planet. It has manifold dimensions: economic, political, security, environmental, health, social, cultural, and others. Globalization has had significant impacts on all economies of the world, with manifold effects. It affects their production of goods and services. It also affects the employment of labour and other inputs into the production process. In addition, it affects investment, both in physical capital and in human capital. It affects technology and results in the diffusion of technology from initiating nations to other nations. It also has major effects on efficiency, productivity and competitiveness (PP. 1, 7). With all that has happened, one can say that Globalization has become an emerging reality. According to Ademola (1998), globalization refers to the increased integration across countries of markets for goods, services and capital (P.107). It implies in turn accelerated expansion of economic activities globally and sharp increases in the movement of tangible and intangible goods across national and regional boundaries. With that movement, individual countries are becoming more closely integrated into the global economy. Their trade linkages and investment flow grow more complex, and cross border financial movements are more volatile. More importantly, globalization has been created, and continues to be maintained by liberation of economic-policies in several key areas. It is clear today that people and nation states can no longer think only in terms of individual states and actions, but, a component of global order. Mahathir (2002) defines globalization as, a word that seems to describe the coming together of all the countries of the globe into one entity. It was conceived by the rich countries, apparently in response to technological advances and the speed and ease of travelling (p.13). Globalization can be said to be the integration of different countries of the world into one global order. With the advent of science and technology, there is an equitable distribution of information of events happening around the globe. This is because people can now communicate, make transactions and meet people in all parts of the world.

Globalization as a concept is all encompassing. It is not only restricted to the economic point of view but also encompasses the political, cultural, religious and other activities of humans. The AWAKE magazine of September 8, 1999, strengthens the above assertion when it posits that; Globalization is more than the flow of money and commodities. It is the growing interdependence of world people and activities through shrinking space, time and disappearing borders. Globalization creates a global village based on shared values. Technology and market integration processes have dominated the world economic system. The world has become a global village as we now see shared values, religions, and even cultures and ideas. The ideological viewpoints of humans are sharpened by the interrelationships that are now domiciled with humans irrespective of their religious, political, economic or cultural groups.

For Murad (2002), globalization exists majorly between developed and developing countries and in most cases, the developed country dominates the developing country's economy, religion, politics and even culture. This is not colonization or imperialism as globalism tends to be subtle and less harmful than the other concepts. Globalization is commonly understood to be a process of change, which comes in many forms. It has a number of direct effects on the economical, political, cultural, religious, social, demographic, environmental and military spheres. Understanding these aspects of globalization is very crucial and important, because the interaction among them can be constructive or destructive. In recent experiences of some developing countries, globalization can trigger security problems, (p. 1).

This can be necessitated by the unnecessary intervention of these developed countries at every slightest security challenge. Sadeeque et al (2015) assert that globalization is not only an opportunity, but, a possibility for underdeveloped nations like Nigeria to shake off the burden and constrain of development by harnessing and utilizing the abundant mineral and human resources in building a pique self reliance economy (p.2). It is also an opportunity that will enhance the political growth of nations as they get to partner and learn the political workings of other countries and improve where and when necessary.

Political globalism is a national policy of treating the whole world as a proper sphere for political influence. African countries have at one point in time or the other been dominated by British or European countries. Before independence, Nigeria's political government was controlled by the British government who made laws that the Nigerian citizens adopted. These influences always happen between developed and developing nations especially countries that feel that they need the assistance of the developed country to run their political affairs.

Sadeeque et al (2015) have also seen globalization as a trend that impacts everyone more and more each day. For centuries, globalization has progressively knitted together the world and created unity out of great diversity (p. 1). This research work takes a cursory look at political globalism and its implication for Africa with particular reference to Nigeria.

Globalism in Africa

Globalism has been a thing of concern for scholars over the years in Africa. While some argue that it has had a tremendous positive effect, others oppose it by seeing it as a concept that has done more harm than good in the African nation. From Sadeeque et al (2015), As trade between far-flung parts of the world produced a global integrated economy, so also ideas, innovation, technology, culture and political philosophy were exported as easily as raw materials. Globalization is an emerging reality (p. 1). It is a reality that cannot be done away with. It is a reality that has come to stay in Africa. In the 1990s 'globalization' has become a particularly fashionable way to analyze changes in the international economy and in the world politics. Advances in technology and modern communications are said to have unleashed new contacts and intercourse among peoples, social movements, transnational corporations, and governments. The result is a set of processes which have affected national and international politics in an extraordinary way (Sadeeque at al 2015, pp. 189-190 citing Ngaire, 2000). Sadeeque at al (2015) further argue that the concept of globalization has attracted debates among scholars in both developed and underdeveloped countries. While proponents argue in favour of globalization, opponents see globalization as another re-colonization of the weaker economies by the stronger nations. Globalization is the movement and integration of the world economies into one entity, by breaking down barriers to free movement of goods, services and capital (p.3). From the economic perspective, Garcia (1998) gives a classical definition of globalization as: Changes in the way production is organized as required by the general dismantling of trade barriers and the free mobility of financial and productive capital, in the context of accelerated technology change...technological development in the sphere of information and electronic services has been a catalyst for speeding the process, bringing about global production distribution and consumption (p.96). From this assertion, globalism in Africa can be said to be viewed as a link through which goods and services are disseminated from one country to another. Globalism was also felt in Africa politically. As globalisation gripped Africa, there was a rise in democracy through multiparty elections in countries like Kenya, Ghana and South Africa. Finally people had the power to elect the people they wanted through the ballot without fear of reprisals. Other countries moved from military dictatorships to civilian rule like Nigeria. Sudan had a referendum to decide its destiny and the vote was final-South Sudan was born.

Political Leadership

According to Chambers Dictionary (1993), political leadership can be seen as a system where there are democratically elected representatives who are vulnerable to de-selection and operate within, as well as influence a constitutional and legal framework. Their source of authority is a mandate: 'permission to govern according to declared policies, regarded as officially granted by an electorate . . . upon the decisive outcome of an election.'

"It is not wise to expect much of political leadership, especially in a democracy" (Firlie, 1968, P. 58). Statements like this abound in contemporary literature on political leadership. However, nowadays, a crisis of confidence seems to emerge between citizens and politicians as people do not just vote for anybody but for who they feel can protect their interest. The particular leadership pacing political systems in Africa can give to us an interesting point of view to understand this phenomenon. To this effect, it becomes paramount for all citizens to understand what define them vis-à-vis their roles in the country they find themselves. The kind of power citizens have in their hands should also give them the chance to determine the positions of their representatives. It is also necessary to understand the roles of politicians elected as representatives and more significantly, to understand the necessity for all of us to have a critical look at what the core components of our societies are. Leaders are the objects of intense admiration in our society, due to their ability to shape the world surrounding them, and their natural capacity to lead and to have malleable followers. Leadership can only be achieved through responsibility and commitment, as "Politics... without belief is impossible" (Mayer, 1950; cit. Gane, 1997 pp. 549-564). The Brothers Karamazov from Fyodor Dostoevsky put forward one explanation as to why leadership is so important: "There are three powers, only three powers on earth, capable of conquering and holding captive forever the conscience of these feeble rebels, for their own happiness –these powers are miracle, mystery, and authority". The possibility to provide all three at the same time is only achievable by those able to grasp the immense complexity of the art of leadership. Political leadership can be put simply as the power given to an individual to manage power. It is the ability to exercise power over people or things.

Weber (1994) focuses his findings on Plato's fundamental question of 'who should rule', therefore, examining the qualities and abilities of the ideal leader. Leadership occupies a central place on the author's rationale, being fundamental for understanding politics. Again the theme of power is what drove Weber's attention, particularly as it is derived from the 'monopoly of legitimate physical violence' allowed in modern states. Therefore, as Weber claims,

> "anyone engaged in politics is striving for power, either power as a means to attain other goals (which may be ideals or selfish in nature), or power for its own sake, which is to say, in order to enjoy the feeling of prestige given by power" (pp. 310-311).

African Political Conflicts

According to Appadorai (2004), man as intoned by Socrates is a social animal. This implies that the gregarious nature of man abhors in all ramifications the idea of isolated life. Therefore, man has to live in a politically organised enclave that is guided by laws. This is imperative because of the insatiability and seemingly selfish nature of man. To begin with, when we observe the life of men around us, we cannot fail to be struck by two facts: as a rule, every man desires to have their own way, to think and act as they like; and at the same time, everyone cannot have his own way, because he lives in society, where one man's desires conflict with those of another. The relations of the individual members of society with one another, therefore, need regulation by government (p.3). In trying to regulate the activities of human beings, a government is formed. This government consist of a body of persons that make decisions relating to the necessity and the essence of rules and regulations guiding our public life. What constitutes the body, the procedures and processes by which the laws are formulated agitated the minds of the political philosophers, whether by the assemblies of the elders (gerontocracy), the committee of the wealthy (plutocracy), the nobles (aristocracy), the experts (technocracy), and the general populace (democracy). This last form of political arrangement appears to be the best form of government (Okonkwo, C. and Felix, N. (2016) citing Okonkwo, 2015 in p. 91).

Africa can be said to be a continent faced with several political imbalances. At every point in time in African countries, there is always a case of political conflicts between one ethnic group and the other or between one political party and the other. Nigeria, for instance, has from time immemorial, battled with political instabilities and enthronement and dethronement. It has been a battle between the civilian and the military government. Democratic forms of governance were generally few and short-lived through the decolonialization and Cold War periods; most African regimes were autocratic and well over half of African regimes were ruled by ethnically-exclusive political elites. We encounter political conflicts at various levels in Africa. From intra-party to inter-party conflict, ethnic clashes, religious political clashes and lots more. Intra-party conflict is the tussles and wrangling within a political party that are inimical to normal nomination and/or election of party flag bearers. It is a conflict that exists between members of the same party either in their clamour for positions or in trying to make their opinions count. Inter-party conflict exists between different political parties. To stress further, Okoli (2001) enumerated factors that are responsible for intra-party opposition as follows: Personality difference, clash of socio-economic interests, ideological incompatibility (P. 3).

To further buttress this, Afegbua (2014) asserts that:

> Conflicts are common and unavoidable in all human society. All over the world, conflicts occur because society is made up of people with differing interests and values. In most societies, conflicts occur when parties in a state of independence perceives divergent views or believe that their aspirations or goals cannot be achieved simultaneously. Therefore, it is only natural that where there is inequality in access to the control of natural resources and political power for instance, there would be discontent, opposition and controversy (p. 1).

Since Nigeria assumed the status of independence, the political parties have been challenged by many conflicts of different dimensions. This as a matter of fact culminated in political instability in the countries. Political ideology is like a superstructure upon which every other thing is built on. It consolidates political party and precedes party structure, organisation and manifesto but when there is a clash of interest, it leads to political conflict. Diversified political ideologies have been one of the major causes of political instability in Africa.

African Political Xenophobia

Hågensen, L. (2014) asserts that fear of the unknown is something one can witness all over the world, and as the movement of people has accelerated with new technologies of transport and communication so has the fear of strangers. This fear of strangers is what we call xenophobia. It derives from two Greek words: *xénos* and *phóbos*, meaning 'stranger' or 'guest' and 'fear', respectively. Consequently xenophobia means fear of the guest or the stranger, though today it has the stronger meaning of hatred of strangers. (p.1). It is not just an African issue alone, just like globalization, every society at one point in time or the other feel insecure with the inflow of immigrants or visitor who will come to fight over human and natural resources with them.

The causes of xenophobia in most African countries particularly South Africa can be discussed in three perspectives. The first is the socio-cultural reason. Here we find social identity theory, which focuses on a person's self-image; this derives from the social group(s) that the individual believes himself/herself to belong to (Tajfel & Turner, 1979, p. 40). As most individuals want to maintain or even enhance their self-image, it is important that the membership' of their group is perceived as something positive. In turn this leads to a need to reject and even express hostility towards the out-group. When this translates into nationalism it becomes a way of promoting one's status as a citizen; this therefore also rejects the foreigner. When a country is going through a political transition, as South Africa has been doing for the last 20 years, nationalism can take the form of hostility towards foreigners and this provides an explanation for xenophobia (Mummendey, Klink & Brown 2001:159-160). The issues of inherited culture can also be linked to this socio-cultural cause of xenophobia.

The second reason can be structural reasons. At this level, we have the relative deprivation theory, the theory of ethnic violence and the group threat theory. Relative deprivation theory suggests that social unrest comes from the perception that one gets less than one is entitled to (Hågensen, L. 2014 Citing Harris, 2002). This can create xenophobic attitudes and practices if the reason for this deficit is believed to be foreigners. It is seen as a zero-sum game where foreigners that have jobs are blamed for unemployment among South Africans (Du Toit & Kotzé 2011, p. 163). In other words the foreigners become 'frustration scapegoats' and this is why xenophobia occurs (Harris, 2002). The theory of ethnic violence by Horowitz (2001), states that external contextual causes in addition to immediate locality-bound causes must be taken into account when looking at violent outbursts. This theory also gives a step-by-step description of how violent ethnic event will unfold (Du Toit & Kotzé 2011, pp. 160-161). It points to causes that were present in South Africa prior to major xenophobic events, and therefore explains what caused these events to take place, thus providing an explanation for xenophobia in the country. Group threat theory suggests that inter-group hostility is largely a reaction to perceived threats from subordinate group(s). If the dominant group finds that its position vis-à-vis the minority group is in jeopardy and fears that it might lose its advantaged social position, hostility can arise (King 2007, p. 1225).

Lastly, xenophobia can be as a result of institutional mismanagement. This consists of the roles of the state. Attitudes and statements from state representatives where they deny xenophobia, or lay blame for crime on foreigners, could generate xenophobia (Bekker, 2010, p. 126). There is also the belief that the government is not doing enough to solve the 'problem' of immigrants (Landau, 2011, p. 13). One can also look at the policies that affect migration into the country. There is a big gap between policy and practice in African countries particularly in South Africa, and this also worsens the xenophobic phenomenon (Bekker, 2010, p. 141). Furthermore Misago (2011) argues that a key trigger for violence against foreign nationals and outsiders in specific locations is localised competition for political and economic power. This competition has kept Africa where it is today. No one wants to serve; everybody wants to be a leader so as to get intoxicated by power.

Effects of Globalism in Africa

Political globalism in Africa has both negative and positive implications. According to Akindele et al (2005),

Africans received globalization naturally with hope. Flows of capital in developing countries would grow promisingly: they were multiplied by six, in six years (from 1990 to 1996). People thought that all men and all countries – would benefit from globalization, which was supposed to help developing countries "create better economic environments', jump into the information age, accelerate development and enhance global harmony.

But this believe did not go down completely well for Africans. The reality, today, is that the globalization of information and communication technology through the use of the internet and satellite images have narrowed and constrained states from taking political actions especially against their citizens without global condemnation or support. For example, the April 14-15, 2014 kidnapping of Chibok girls and the reluctance of the former President Goodluck Ebele Jonathan administration to take action, gave birth to global condemnation and the 'bringbackourgirls movement' in Nigeria and across the globe, forcing the government to accept responsibility and promise to take action in rescuing the girls, even though the whole episode looked improperly-stage-managed. Such is the powers and interconnectivity of the globe today, thereby eroding political sovereignty (Sadeeque et al, 2015. P.3). As a result of globalization, most African countries cannot comfortably take decisions without the globe being either fully or partially aware or involved in it. The breakthrough in information technology has broken down barriers and enhanced the world interaction by collapsing it into what we now refer to as the global village. Thereby, presenting African countries and their political governments unclothed. Today, information spreads like wild fire disseminating both true and false stories.

Also, globalism has helped positively to bring the world together. Politically, leaders in different countries hold meetings and conferences which are meant to benefit their citizens and during the course of such meetings and conferences, innovations which are meant to boost the political, social and economic life of the general public are introduced.

Conclusion

According to Sadeeque et al, (2015),

"The world economic and political arrangement is a single social community. This social community is a mix of wealth and poverty, progress and despair, exploitation and assistance, dependence and interdependence. For sure, some countries are rich and some others are rather poor. The rich countries have certain common characteristics. They are economically prosperous, politically stable, socially harmonious and technologically sophisticated. Given the link between politics and economics, the rich countries are very competitive in international trade and exchange relations, while in contrast, poor countries are in the majority, and are characteristically backward in economics, unstable in politics, socially disharmonious and technologically dependent" (p.3).

For the poor countries of Africa, globalization has changed the pattern of international economic relations. The new pattern is to promote growth in the motive force for globalize economic system. It has been argued by both proponents and antagonists of the global drives for globalization, that the new doctrine is facilitating a lot of crises and conflicts in the world. This has made many scholars and leaders alike to argue that globalization has not only created more crises but has also complimented in deepening inequality and underdevelopment (Sadeeque et al, 2015, p. 4). This clearly shows the need for complementality of countries to help build the political, economical, sociological power of other countries especially the developing countries. Political globalism needs to be embraced to be in the growth of other smaller countries but this should not be an opportunity to exploit them. Undoubtedly, globalization has created more problems than solving the existing ones. Therefore, the challenge before countries like Nigeria is on how to re-position the economy through diversification and building the capacity of her citizens to visualize, theorize, innovate and develop the critical skills and spirit for national growth and development

Recommendations

I recommend the following:

1. African countries should build policy thrust to protect and enhance her industrial growth and development especially in harnessing and utilizing the huge human demography at her disposal.
2. There should be a creative utilization of the human and natural resources as there is a general believe that, creative utilization of the human being is the engine of growth and development. This will in turn liberate them from being parasites and thorns on the skins of other countries. What make growth and development happen in any society, is the ability of individuals and groups to imagine, theorize, conceptualize, experiment, invent, articulate and manage problems and do hundred things with their minds and hands that contribute to the progress of the individual and the society in general (Sadeeque et al 2015 citing Harrison, 1985).

3. Most people today in Africa aspire to higher standard of living, longer lives and fewer health problems, education for themselves and their children that will increase their earning capacity and leave them more in control of their lives (Sadeeque et al, 2015, p. 5). This opportunity should be created by the government of African countries.

4. Developed countries should be made to play only advisory and supportive roles and not to impose orders on the developing countries.

5. Political decisions should be based on consensus and the interest of the general public should be taken into consideration when the government make policies.

References

Ademola, O. (1998) as cited in Akpuru-Aja, A (2001). Selected themes in international economic relations: Understanding trends of globalization and regionalization. Enugu, Rhycee Kerex Publishers.

Afegbua, I. (2014). Conflicts and political instability in nigeria: Causes, concequences and prospects. Viewed http://chrisdonasco.blogspot.com.ng/2014/12/conflicts-and-political-instability-in.html. Accessed 17 August, 2017

Akindele, S. T. et al (2002). "Globalisation, its implications and consequences for Africa". http://globalization.icaap.org/content/v2.1/ 01_akindele_etal.html. Accessed 19 August, 2017.

Aluko, S. (2007). Reforming Nigeria: Which model? The economic dimension: Being a paper presented at the 2nd Trust Annual Dialogue, organized by Media Trust, Abuja.

Appadorai, A. (2004). The substance of politics. New Delhi India: Oxford University Press.

Bekker, S. (2010).' Explaining violence against foreigners and strangers in urban South Africa: outburst during May and June 2008', in A. A. Yusuf (Ed.). *The African Yearbook of International Law*. Leiden: Brill Publishers: 125-149.

Brittan, L. (1998). Globalisation vs sovereignty? The European response. The 1997 Rede Lecture and Related Speeches. Cambridge: Cambridge University Press.

Du Toit, P. & Kotzé, H. (2011). Liberal democracy and peace in South Africa. New York: Palgrave Macmillan.

Gane, N. (1997). "Weber on the ethical irrationality of political leadership". Sociology 31(3): 549-564.

Hågensen, L. (2014). Understanding the causes and the nature of xenophobia in South Africa: A case study of De Doorns. Stellenbosch University http://scholar.sun.ac.za. Accessed 19th August, 2017.

Harshe, R. (Ed) (2004). Interpreting globalization: Perspectives in international relations, New Delhi: Rawat Publications.

Harris, B. (2002). 'Xenophobia: A new pathology for a new South Africa?', in D. Hook & G. Eagle (Eds.). Psychopathology and Social Prejudice. Cape Town: University of Cape Town Press.

Horowitz, D. (2001). The deadly ethnic riot. Berkeley and Los Angeles: University of California Press.

Intriligator, M. D. (2003). "Globalization of the world economy: Potential benefits and costs and a net assessment", policy brief, No 33, January, Milken Institute: University of California, Los Angeles.

King, R. D. (2007). 'Group threat and social control: Race, perceptions of minorities and the desire to punish'. Social forces.

Landau, L. B. (Ed.) (2011). 'Introducing the demons', in Landau, L.B. (Ed.). Exorcising the demons within: Xenophobia, violence and statecraft in contemporary South Africa. Johannesburg: Wits University Press.

Mahathir, M. (2002). Globalization and the new realities. Putrajaya: Pelanduk Publication.

Mayer, J. (1950). Max Weber and German politics: A study in political sociology. London: Faber and Faber.

Misago, J. (2011). 'Disorder in a changing society: Authority and the micro-politics of violence', in L. B. Landau (Ed.). Exorcising the demons within: Xenophobia, violence and statecraft in contemporary South Africa.Johannesburg: Wits University Press.

Mummendey, A., Klink, A. & Brown, R. (2001). 'Nationalism and patriotism: National identification and Outgroup rejection'. *British Journal of Social Psychology*, PP. 159-172

Ngaire, W (2000). "The political economy of globalization". In W. Ngaire (Ed). The political economy of globalization. Basingstoke: Macmillan.

Okoli, A. C. (2001). "The political economy intra-party opposition in Anambra State (1999-2001)". B.Sc. Project submitted to the Department of Political Science, Nnamdi Azikwe University, Awka .

Okonkwo, C. & Felix, N. (2016). Intra-party conflict and prospects of democratic consolidation. In Nigeria. IOSR *Journal Of Humanities And Social Science* (IOSR-JHSS) Volume 21, Issue 5, Ver. 3 (May. 2016). www.iosrjournals.org. Accessed 15th August, 2017.

Sadeeque, A., Suleiman, B., & Bukhari B, (2015). Globalization and Nigeria's quest for self-Reliance and Political sovereignty: Changing the Narratives. International Journal of Humanities and Social Science Invention ISSN (Online): 2319 – 7722, ISSN (Print): 2319 – 7714 www.ijhssi.org. Accessed 15th August, 2017.

Schwarz, C. (Ed) (1993), Chambers dictionary, Edinburgh: Chambers Harrap,

Tajfel, H. & Turner, J. C. (1979). 'An integrative theory of intergroup conflict.' In W. G. Austin, & S. Worchel (Eds.). *The Social Psycology of Intergroup Relations Monterey*. CA: Brooks/Cole.

Weber, M. (1994). "The profession and vocation of politics". In P. Lassman & R. Speirs (Eds.) Weber-Political Writings. New York: Cambridge University Press.

CHAPTER NINE

RELIGIOUS PLURALISM AND ITS PSYCHO-PHILOSOPHICAL APPROACH AND RELEVANCE

Philip Osarobu ISANBOR

Executive Summary

With the upsurge of religious intolerance, violence and conflict, and coping with conflicting and disharmony of religious beliefs and imposition of false or faulty doctrines and foreign faiths, there is an urgent need to check or re-evaluate the modes, practice and absurdity of religious convictions which are plausibly evidenced in the domain of religious fanaticism and fundamentalism. With conflicts, peace and justice are denied, and if these are not realised, meaningful development is utopic, even when God is called upon. Hence, the paper explicated the valuation of religious pluralism which seems to suggest the accommodation of religious freedom and tolerance of beliefs or convictions that are situated in the respect of human rights and dignity. In religious freedom, God is expressed in faith and worship in accordance with individual conviction and understanding of the "Beingness" and personhood of God. The paper concluded that adherents of religions should allow the thriving of religious pluralism with its ingredients of religious freedom and respect for human rights and dignity against the weighty negative effects of religious fanaticism and fundamentalism, all for the attainment of integral human development that promotes the religiosity of the wholeness of human person.

Background: Considering the Value of Religion

The study of religion shows the nature and attitude of humanity toward the worship of the Supreme Deity, object or a particular ideology that it believes on. This has brought us to the understanding of our interest, purpose and closeness to certainty on that particular reverential entity which we believe in and willing to convince others to follow by our outward and inward enthusiastic mentality in the light of salvation and earthly wellbeing. We discuss the weights of religion on human development have been vast because there are a lot of violence of human rights, freedom and dignity, even as a result of the practice of religion. As Kimball (2008) asserts that;

> *The record of human history shows that noble acts of love, self-sacrifice, and service to others are frequently rooted in deeply held religious worldviews. At the same time, history clearly shows that religion has often been linked to the worst examples of human behaviour. It is somewhat trite, but nevertheless sadly true that more wars have been waged, more people killed, and these days more evil perpetuated in the name of religion than by any other institutional force in human history* (p. 87).

Many interests have being invested to monitor these development and to wright the aberrations, so that there will be meaningful integral development. It is contemporarily certain now that we recognising that our destructive behaviour is always an outgrowth of incongruence. That is, we do destructive things when we are out of touch, rather than in touch, with our authentic self (Kimball 2008, 50). That is, a communal humanity. On this course of action and interest for integral human development through proper internalization of religion, Benedict XVI (2011, no. 13) explicates that;

> *despite the lessons of history and the efforts of states, international and regional organizations, non-governmental organizations and the many men and women of good will who daily work to protect fundamental rights and freedoms, today's world also witnesses cases of persecution, discrimination, acts of violence and intolerance based on religion.*

This is emphatically about the faulty promotion of religious fanaticism and fundamentalism. On the contrary, it should be taken that man is fundamentally religious. But human religiosity should be aimed at promoting a sound spiritual relationship with its Creator and fellow creatures. To achieve this feat is by upholding some values of justice, love and fairness in his dealing with them. The constant effort to achieve this situation leads to mutual understanding and tolerance, especially in a multi-cultural and pluri-religious society like Nigeria (Ukaonu 2013, 35). This is about wrong internalization of religious conviction, vesting it imposingly, as an act of indoctrination upon others. And then, Campbell (1971, 27) observes that;

> *Those who come to believe that their own radical beliefs are so unacceptable as to constitute irreligion may in fact be mistaken, and a wider knowledge of their own religious tradition may later lead them to the realisation that they have been espousing an acceptable, if unorthodox, interpretation of the faith.*

The aim of the paper is to understand the effectual reality of religious fanaticism, fundamentalism and pluralism. This is to relate these concepts in understanding religion itself more properly. One needs the proper assessment on the causes of the multiplicity of religious groups or sects and their assessable investigation of their system in relation to societal peace and harmony. In the history of man, religion has been a very part of his life, so man cannot do without religion or been religious. Man is at the middle of God and nature.

All religions of the world are in one way or the other pointing to the fact that human beings do not, and cannot, stand alone, that they are related to and dependent on powers external and beyond them. Broadly put therefore, religion is a belief based on a person's ultimate relation to the universe, to a god or gods (Okelezo and Nwosu 2008). The religious quality of man is highly needed to maintain this relationship, which everything is channel to reverence the Supreme Being and for the wellbeing of the existing realities, including man.

Now, the psycho-philosophical study of religious fanaticism and fundamentalism will make us to understand the propelling force of interest in humanity, which makes him/her behaves in certain ways which classified him/her to be a religious fanatic, and why he adopts the belief system and conviction with great enthusiastic spirit. Psychology is the science for the study of mind and behaviour of the human person will lead us to accept the facts that there are always propelling forces and interests for such developments. The relevance of this discipline cut across all works of life, and which religion is not an exception.

Using philosophical coloration, this paper will necessarily lead us to assess the understanding of human person in relation to the outcomes of its religious conviction, especially conflicts that ensue from its fanaticism and fundamentalism. We remembered that Benedict XVI has aligned his interest for global harmony with the thrust of religious freedom, and he said that, "in a particular way, in Asia and in Africa, the chief victims are the members of religious minorities, who are prevented from freely professing or changing their religion by forms of intimidation and the violation of their rights, basic freedoms and essential goods, including the loss of personal freedom and life itself" (2011, no. 13). Benedict XVI believes that the easiest way to achieve global harmony is mainly through the workability of religious tolerance and the positive exactness of religious freedom. It is obvious that there are negative results of religious fanaticism and fundamentalism in the face of religious conflicts. But there is need to understand the effects of religious fundamentalism and fanaticism, and in relation to pluralism

Clarifying Terms and their Explanatory Objective Notations

Here, for the purpose of the comprehensive grasping to the tenet of the discourse, we clarify some concepts in some details. They are: religious fanaticism, religious fundamentalism and religious pluralism.

Religious Fundamentalism: the word "fundamentalism" is derived from the word 'fundamental' which means the basic, serious and important parts of something. But fundamental in relation to religion is defined as "the practice of following very strictly the basic rules and teachings of any religion, most especially, as in, dogmatically." Religious Fundamentalism and dogmatism are seen to be the same. Both are centred on the teachings and doctrines of a particular sect or religion in which an individual belongs and hopes to uphold the teachings and doctrines strictly. With the words for the advocacy and solicitation of peace, Benedict XVI affirms that;

> *It should be clear that religious fundamentalism and secularism are alike in that both represent extreme forms of a rejection of legitimate pluralism and the principle of secularity. Both absolutize a reductive and partial vision of the human person, favouring in the one case forms of religious integralism and, in the other, of rationalism. A society that would violently impose or, on the contrary, reject religion is not only unjust to individuals and to God, but also to itself. God beckons humanity with a loving plan that, while engaging the whole person in his or her natural and spiritual dimensions, calls for a free and responsible answer which engages the whole heart and being, individual and communitarian.*

Also, the views of Peter Clarks (1982) on the issues of religious fundamentalism is understood as a long term religious methodology of interest, which although very selfish or sectional, when he asserts that;

> *With the expansion and development of Islamic education system, of literary in Arabic, and the more frequent contacts with the Muslim world of North Africa and the middle East brought about by the pilgrimage, study abroad and increasing supply of book and writing on Islam, an increasing number of Muslims in West Africa in areas with a long tradition of Islam.*

The above assertion or observation was on Islamic religion, and which could be likening to other religions as well. Religion fundamentalism lies on the placidity of belief of an individual, which other religious are not excluded. This is basically on the attitude of the religious participants, when we limit God by our own restricted understanding we often are conformed to this world. We are trying to force the Lord into the mould of our limited knowledge whether it is based upon our education and science or our interpretation of the scriptures. This is the problem of dogmatic perception of God, limiting the freedom of human intellect in the perceptive multiplicity of realities.

Religious Fanaticism: Fanaticism is the belief in politics, religion, or other areas that greatly exceeds the norm in enthusiasm and includes a willingness to sacrifice all else to realise its ends. Religious fanaticism is a state of "wild and excessive religious" mentality with great enthusiasm. Fanatics in the context of this discourse too, are the religious adherents who hold tenaciously to the absolute truth claims of the founder of their religions and ensure that such claims are maintained and never diluted (Atoi 2013). According to psychologists; religious fanaticism is a psychological deviant behaviour since it is always tends as negative factor against peaceful environment of the people. The notion of religious fanaticism is on the nature of the relationship between God and man, and how man has interpreted it. Reiterating the thought of Mala, Ubruvhre affirms the propelling conviction of religious fanatics, that;

To them, the belief in a religion other than theirs runs foul of the injunctions handed down through a messenger or prophet as the case may be. The fanatics see other "believers" as those who have gone astray and who need some sermon or preaching to make them fall in line with their doctrine, which to them is always the best and most reliable basis for redemption on the judgment day.... They believe rather wrongly that those who do not share their mode of worship or the doctrine of their religion were better dead than alive.

More succinctly, on the same platform, Omoregbe (2002) points that; "religious fanaticism is the product of ethnocentricity and narrow-mindedness which prevents the fanatic from 'seeing that there is no essential difference between what he is doing and what the other person is doing, no essential difference between his own religion and of the other person." So, he is psychologically stereotype and philosophically and sociologically limited and imbalance in accessing his religious sentiment. This was in the line of thought with Baum (1975) that;

Even classical theology was well that despite its highly conceptual understanding of revelation and faith, what really counted was the vital assimilation of religious truth. In scholasticism this was expressed by insisted that faith must be alive with hope and love before it mediate divine justification.

Consolidating this psychological conviction of position, Fredrick Feuerbach expounded that; this conviction on the assimilation of religious truth was that it was not God who created man; rather man has succeeded in creating God in his mind in images he likes God to be seen, for there was no such God. And he said that; the reason why God has always been seen to be the superior is that man himself as incapacitated in the light of natural forces and human power. And man in that estranged state turned all his wishes/ desires to God. It was man who created God in man's image. So, the object of religion is dictated by man in his psychological conviction on whom or what he considers God to be. Now it is time to dismantle that oppressive fabrication of man, for man to be liberated, has created psychic fixation to be fanatic in his conviction.

Religious Pluralism: With the development of human mentality towards the transcendent, there is simultaneous polarisation of other religions, on which background, David Moberg in his book *Wholistic Christianity,* published in 1985; associated polarisation of religion with: accompanied by selective church membership as people gravitate towards the religious groups that stress whatever they believe to be the 'correct' position on issues that they believe are crucial. Before now, just like the trends of humanism, it was a revolt against the monopoly of theology and church dogma in the theory and practice of medieval life. It was not directed not directed against Christianity, on the contrary. Humanism accepted its close connection with the Christian tradition and Christian morality. The universal validity of Christian teaching and its international character was taken by humanists as the foundation of their ideas. In its original setting humanism meant the liberation of reason form the shackles of dogma and a critical study of nature and humanity through and observation of actual facts (Mistra, Sharma and Bernsal 2007, 5).

Religious plurality is the situation in a globalising world that helps to create, brings together traditions with irreconcilable differences. Understandably, the modern mind is bemused with this unsettling politico-religious diversity, hence the growing suspicion with institutionalised religion (Selmanovic, 2009). Religious pluralism presupposes or suggests religious freedom. Only in freedom can man direct himself toward goodness (Vatican II Council, *Gaudium et spes*, 17). Even nature respect the freedom of man and it expects him to be responsive. To be responsive means that he has to manage his freedom in order to maintain the person's freedom. Men can understand themselves properly only in reference to the relationship established between them at the time of his creation. Being created in His image, God places man in that special relationship with him; and enters into a partnership with man by entrusting the whole created world to his care. Man effectively becomes the presence of the Creator in the world (Kusumalayam 2008, 195). It behoves on man to make good use of his reason and associates it with the application of freedom. At the same time, two categories become increasingly central to the idea of progress: reason and freedom.

For Benedict XVI, progress is primarily associated with the growing dominion of reason, and this reason is obviously considered to be a force of good and a force for good. Progress is the overcoming of all forms of dependency—it is progress towards perfect freedom. Likewise freedom is seen purely as a promise, in which man becomes more and more fully himself. In both concepts—freedom and reason—there is a political aspect (2007, no.18). In another occasion, Benedict XVI (2009, no. 56) goes further to assert;

> *Denying the right to profess one's religion in public and the right to bring the truths of faith to bear upon public life has negative consequences for true development. The exclusion of religion from the public square — and, at the other extreme, religious fundamentalism — hinders an encounter between persons and their collaboration for the progress of humanity. Public life is sapped of its motivation and politics takes on a domineering and aggressive character. Human rights risk being ignored either because they are robbed of their transcendent foundation or because personal freedom is not acknowledged. Secularism and fundamentalism exclude the possibility of fruitful dialogue and effective cooperation between reason and religious faith.*

This act of stewardship demands that man should not be violent to what entrusted to him, including himself, because the Creator does not intend him to mismanage anything, but to be humane with nature and explore, not to exploit, the gifts in/of nature for his comfort and development. This is the bedroom of developmental peace which humanity cannot but do with. Yet it should be added that, as well as religious fanaticism that in some contexts impedes the exercise of the right to religious freedom, so too the deliberate promotion of religious indifference or practical atheism on the part of many countries obstructs the requirements for the development of peoples, depriving them of spiritual and human resources.

Psychology of Religious Fundamentalism and Fanaticism

There will be always the connection of human' psychological state of mind or his mental conviction to his level of religious development, rather than its religiosity. The question about God's existence and the internalization of His attributes can also contribute to such psychological development, and if not properly channelled to respect other people's conviction; may be lead to mental and social debasement, which may be classified as religious fanaticism and fundamentalism, even the culture of religious bigotry and particularism. On this, Carl Jung observes that; "they offer their soul to God, but do not know what they are doing and never have known. They do it, motivated by the same preconscious archetype which the ancient Egyptians, on their monuments, who to the sun worshipping dog-headed baboon, albert in full knowledge that this ritual gesture was in honour of God" (Jung 1997, 471-452). From the assertion by Carl Jung, who based his observation on human behaviour towards religions and its involvement, and which support the notion of Sigmund Freud in his psychoanalytic theory, he is of the opinion with great conviction that religious behaviour of a man is traceable to the personality development at the phallic stages in personality formation as a result of Oedipus and Electra complex as the case may be. As Baum (1975, 244) explicates;

> For vast numbers of people in western culture, the Oedipal story is still a central model of self-knowledge and personal deliverance, nevertheless by investing the story with universal validity, orthodox Freudian psychoanalysis become an ideology that subjects people to a preconceived image and possibly imprisons then in a false imagination.

So the tendency to rectify the failure has crated in the psyche of man a patriarchal reverence of God whom he claimed to be his Supreme Being and develop the fanatic mentality to be faithful to Him and never to fail Him again, which he had done in his phallic stage. In this, Sheen affirmed that; "your false sense of guilt is due to an Oedipus complex if you are a man and an Electra complex if you are a woman." Thus, many of the psychologists supported this viewpoint which was developed from Freudian theory of psychoanalysis, and believed that religious fanaticism is bore out of it and the freedom of man to believe anything and holds on to it brings the religious complexity and psyche mentality to religiously faithful to his belief system, and ever ready to convince others to do and behave the same way. In the light of this, Maurus (2007, 136) supported the works of John W. Young and Rene Descartes, on the religion and its psychological mentality, and the human consciousness towards it, and he said;

> Yet our experience of everything is partial. It means the reality of human limits and human brokenness. We have a taste for the infinite and the hole. We are finite with a limitless openness that can be filed only by our surrender to God.

The mind-set is out of the hope which resides in man on his God, whether the hope is faulty or not, deceptive or realistic, man believes the end period of the earthly events will be positive if he is faithful to the end of time, or suddenly when he died. So the fear not to miss hopeful end, brings about his animalistic nature of him to be dogmatic in his religious thinking and be fanatic in his religious actions and participation. Carl Jung (p. 449) vehemently stated that; "it remains blissfully unaware of the philosophically surmise, and is convinced that with this opinion it has established the essential *instinctuality* of all psychic processes." This philosophical assertion in the study of human religious mentality was supported by Sheen, who approached it from a theological angle, and believes that;

The supreme adventure is religion. By religion is not meant the sterile sitting in comfortable pew, but the response to the promise of the God-man, I have come that you may have life and have it more abundantly. That is the point- more abundantly; it challenges us to liquidate our unruly wills, our egocentrism, our petty search for aloneness, and our selling a field to buy the pearl of great price. This adventure loves not the spark but the flame.

Since man is hopeful creature and he believed that he does have power to save himself form any predicaments and he cannot derive peace all by himself, he seems to be religiously fixated, on which Karl Marx asserted that: "religion is the sigh of the oppressed, and religion is the opium of the people." This disposition is on human conviction that all hopes should be based on the supremacy of God and less to his own ability. Again in an abortive protest, Marx has it that the crime of religion and God is that they have canonised man's suffering which could have been avoided. He was not trying to condemn religion totally but the attitude of man in which he has resign his fate to his God to be of help and dispensable solution to his problems; and ever ready to worship and reverence Him as long he believes his solutions come. This was the background for his dictum: Religion is the opium of the people.

The Check on Religious Fundamentalism and Fanaticism

The check is based on what we conceived religions to be, especially in the social, ethical and spiritual development of humanity. It should be taken in line with thoughts of Cooper and Epperson (2008) that;

> *Unlike Freud ad Marx, we do not believe that religion is intrinsically destructive, neurotic or a distraction from social change. Yet like Freud and Marx, we believe that religion should be asked rigorous questions concerning its own healthiness. We do not believe that simply because persons claim to be religious that they are necessarily more ethical, more righteous, or more holy than their secular counterparts. Healthy religious commitment will manifest itself in healthy attitudes and behaviour towards others.*

For the reason that there are structures which at least implicitly open up the range of meaning beyond the confines of a closed religious system (Robley 1971, 151) and since anything can be questioned with contemporary inquisitive mind-set that guarantees private or individualistic conviction, there is need for checks of such development. According to relativist culture, the individuals acquire their own "truth" and "reality" solely from their specific culture. Simply disagreeing with someone else's point of view or questioning their moral values are seen as judgmental and intolerant. Those who evangelize on behalf of a particular religion are said to be 'imposing their narrow beliefs on others. This is basically the primary of religious pluralism. According to the Fathers of the Vatican II Council in the Document for the Declaration of Religious Liberty (*Dignitatis humanae*), it should be accepted that;

Contemporary man is becoming increasingly conscious of the dignity of the human person; more and more people are demanding that men should exercise fully their own judgment and a responsible freedom in their action and should not be subject to the pressure of coercion but inspired by a sense of duty.

From the very before, contemporary developmental conditions posit that we should understand that the cause of religious pluralism are traceable to the: struggle for leadership; involvement in competition between the ideas by false and true teachings; question of conducts and ideological supremacy; issue of personnel appointments; scruples over convictions about diet or other details of personal morality; elements of religious systems of little religious understanding and agreeable explanation; and linkage of religious and political ideas. On these grounds, religious pluralism is constantly ne dynamic, that is on-going especially in the generation of individuals who are very sensitive to the quest of power, liberation, individualism, supremacy, acquisition of wealth and of recognition and possessed by the spirit of the talked-dog syndrome.

Religious pluralism is mostly and recently seen in this modern society as the manifestation of churches especially under Christianity and been classified as Pentecostalism, which are prominent in Western Europe and Africa. The other phase of religious pluralism is the development of distinctive religious sects or groups. The manifestation of religious is outcome from the individualistic spirituality and in most recent cases as a result of social interest among the reason of religious pluralism given initially. The check will be on the decentralization of a particular belief system as claimed by particular set of individuals of the same mind-set of religiosity, on the attainment of salvation and blessings form the supreme deity.

So, "religious pluralist's check is very much evident in the redundancy of the speed of religious fundamentalism on the part of diehard religious individual who believed their faith and religion only possess the truth of salvation and liberation" (Wilson, Ibid). All religions are directed to achieve the same goal which is to worship the Supreme Being, in peaceful and loving conviction, the effect of religious pluralism has checkmated the excessiveness of religious fundamentalism and fanaticism in general aspect of religious feeling, when the human religious freedom is respected. In this Bryan Wilson asserted that each religion has becomes a continual check to others, he posits that;

> *The jealous god of Judaism, and subsequently of Christianity and Islam, provided directives for the prescription for social order.…. In comparison, eastern religions provided no such social dynamic. The passivity of Buddhism and the indeterminacy and tolerance of Hinduism, and the lack of sustained zeal in proselytizing, appear to bear a relationship to the absence of that rigour which monotheism has encouraged in western religion.*

More straightforwardly, there is a great need for proper religious pluralism on the ground on the increase of existing religions of different belief systems and approaches in relationships to the convinced supreme Deity. On this, the Vatican II Council Fathers (1965) posit that; "it is largely because of more frequent contacts with each other; men have become aware of pluralism and indeed have come to see it as the hallmark of our age. True pluralism, however, is impossible unless men and communities of different origins and culture undertake dialogue." For the purpose of ecclesiological emphasis, the Vatican II Council Fathers go further to assert that: "it is demanded by the dynamic course of action which is changing the face of modern society. It is demanded by the pluralism of society, and by the maturity man has reached in this day and age..., and to conduct a dialogue with dignity." It could be ascertained that amidst the growing numbers of religions, there is a necessity of distinctive qualities of any religions to show its uniqueness, and channel them towards attaining the needed understanding of other religions.

Psycho-Philosophical Consideration of Religious Pluralism on Present Humanity

The whole process of human socialisation must be properly internalised and ordered. It must involve the avoidance of religious fanaticism and fundamentalism. Religious tenets must be fully integrated to avoid religious, social and environmental frictions. Religion has been the product of man's existence, and it has been one of his major tools of social and spiritual integrations, if and when properly adopted (see, Wankar 2015 and Otonko 2015). The central message of any religion is on peace, love and the avoidance of conflicts among humans which the founder of any religion had taught his/ her followers for the attainment for happy end.

The goal of every religion should be permanently ordered along the respect of natural law with universal morality which is to "do good and avoid evil". With this, peace and justice have become stills that must be acquired by every individual who desires the symbiotic living, limiting the culture of conflicts and violence, even in the name of faulty religious convictions (Fasuyi and Isanbor 2014). The patrimony of principles and values expressed by an authentic religiosity is a source of enrichment for peoples and their *ethos*. It speaks directly to the conscience and mind of men and women, it recalls the need for moral conversion, and it encourages the practice of the virtues and a loving approach to others as brothers and sisters, as members of the larger human family (Benedict XVI 2011, no. 9). The concern of man is the concern of the human family. The development of humanness of man is the presupposition of the development of the human family, and this development must be sustained for integral growth of human society, even in the domain of religion.

Here, the enduring words of Shakespeare come to mind: "strong reasons make strong actions." This is about man's behavioural tendency. Now that the nature of man is understood to be hopeful being, which has sharpen his thinking and to be religiously rigorous in finding solutions to his problems and most of the time relying on God for his pitiable state of living, his religious mentality will remain fanatic always. The fanatic approach to God is based on his hopeless state of his life, so he tends to please the belief that will help to achieve that which he cannot get on his own. So he places every necessary apparatus to worship that the figure irrespectively what people interpret his action to be, and try to coarse to embrace the same methodology. In modern times phenomenology and hermeneutics have proposed a radically new philosophical approach to the phenomenon of religion, which refuses to philosophically "surmount" it; this trend attempts to interpret religion by tracing its inner logic, its specific invariants and language, its attitude to humanity.

Researchers so far have found shortcomings in these new approaches, in which - they believe - the philosophical horizon is lost. These authors stress the imperative need for a multi-dimensional approach to the complexity of religion; that the principle of religious pluralism should be grounded through a philosophical approach that transcends specific religions; and that, on this basis, an "ethics of dialogue" between religions should be built, of the kind that could hardly be achieved in the framework of the separate branches of specialized study of religion, nor within the limits of theology, which is usually connected with a specific religion (Bogomilova 2007, 60). Obviously, the changes and varieties in religion due to pluralism are very pronounced. Religious fundamentalism should be seen as been decentralised and put in check by the approaches developed and yet to actualise the needed principles in religions.

Evaluative Conclusion

From the foregoing, it should be understood or adopted that religious pluralism is a necessary or better "evil" for the check of the negative effects of religious fanaticism and fundamentalism. It is when the adherents of religions understand the importance of religious freedom that we will understand the true tenets of religions- which are peace, justice and love (charity), all cumulate ultimately to the attainment of salvation. The psychic- philosophical consideration of human religiosity sought that the true religiosity should accommodate the psychological and spiritual growth and conviction of others, in freedom, common good and love.

More straightforwardly, religious pluralism presupposes the adaptation of religious freedom. It is the willingness to express one's conviction without coercion. It should be understood that no single model of religion can accommodate the multiplicity of human intellectual veracity of interest and human religious vitality of transcendental projection, all towards the knowledgeable relationship with their creator- God. This is due to vast population of humanity and it will be monotonous if everyone is under singular religious modelling. This is because, it is in variety of purpose and conviction that the *Beingness* of God is universally expressed or known, and even these varieties, God remain fully unknown. That is He is God, not any other referential being. With religious pluralism or plurality, the perceptive varieties of the *Beingness* of God are envisaged, and the beauty of such development should be expressed in purposeful freedom.

References

Akomolafe, A. C. & Usifoh, E. E. (2014). Pluralism of Spiritual Transformation and Moral Change: Heralds of a New Opportunity for Social Action. *Enwisdomization Journal*, 6(1), 46-78.

Atoi, N. E. (2013). The Philosophy of Religious Pluralism and the Security Question in Nigeria. *Department of Religious Studies: Biannual International Religious Studies Conference.* University of Ibadan, Ibadan, 14-17th May.

Benedict XVI (2005). *Spe Salvi.* VC: Libreria Editrice Vaticana

Benedict XVI (2007). *Message for the World day of Peace.* VC: Libreria Editrice Vaticana.

Benedict XVI (2009). *Caritas in Veritate.* VC: Libreria Editrice Vaticana.

Benedict XVI (2011). *Message for the World Day of Peace.* VC: Libreria Editrice Vaticana.

Baum, G. (1975). *Religion and Alienation: a Theological Reading of Sociology.* New York: Paulist Press.

Bogomilova, N. (2012). Philosophical Approaches to Religion in the Perspective of the Concept of Human Essence. *Postmodernism Problems*, 2(1), 54-60.

Campbell, C. (1971). *Towards a Sociology of Irreligion.* London: The Macmillan Press

Comblin, J. (1989). *The Holy Spirit and Liberation.* NY: Burns & Oates.

Cooper, T. D. and Epperson, C. K. (2008). *Evil: Satan, Sin and Psychology.* Mumbai: St Paul Press.

Ekstrom, R. R. (2002). *The New Concise Catholic Dictionary.* Mumbai: St Paul Press.

Feuerbach, L. (1957). *The Essence of Christianity.* NY: Harper Torch Books.

Fasuyi, A. O. and Isanbor, P. O. (2014). Educating Socio-philosophical Nature of Religion for National Symbiotic living, *Enwisdomization Journal*, 6(1), pp. 23-45.

Isanbor, P. O. (2012). Evaluation of the Meaning and Working of Religion. *The Social Scientist*, 2(1), 78-86.

Flannery, A. (ed, 2004). *Vatican II Council documents.* Mumbai: St Paul.

Jung, C. G. (1997). *Selected Writings.* NY: Bollingen Foundation.

Kimball, C. (2002). *When Religion Becomes Evil.* San Francisco: Harper San Francisco.

Maurus, J. (2007). *Make the Most of your Potential.* Mumbai: Better Yourself Books

Mistra, R. C., Sharma, P. and Bernsal, H. (2007). *International Encyclopaedia of education*, Vol. 2. New Delhi: APH Publication.

Moberg, O. D. (1985). *Wholistic Christianity.* Elgin: Brethren Press.

Okelezo, S. and Nwosu, W. (2008). Religion and the Human Quest for Pleasure. *Apostolos Magazine*, Vol. 6, pp. 6-8.

Otonko, J. O. (2015). Rethinking our Togetherness as Nigerians in the Face of Crises: Towards Nation Building. *The Aquinas Journal*, Vol. 7, pp. 67-89.

Peter, C. B. (1982). *West Africa and Islam.* London: Edward Arnold Ltd.

Robley, W. E. (1971). *The Coming Convergence of World Religion.* NY: Newman Press.

Selmanovic, S. (2009). *It's all Really about God: Reflections of a Muslim Atheist Jewish Christian.* San Francisco, CA: Jossey-Bass.

Sheen, F. J. (2004). *Guide to Contentment.* Mumbai: St Paul Press.

Ubrurhe, J. O. (2000). The Integrative and Disintegrative Functions of Religion: The Nigerian Experience. In S. U. Erivwo and M. P. Adogbo (eds). *Contemporary Essays in the Study of Religions.* Lagos: Fairs and Exhibitions.

Ukaonu, A. E. (2013). Nostra Aetate and the Necessity of Dialogue in Nigeria's Unending Religious Crisis. *West African Journal of Ecclesial Studies*, Vol. 10, pp. 22-37.

Ukwamadua, N. (2005). God and the Question of his Existence: the Panacea of Pantaleon Iroegbu. In G. Ukagba (ed). *Philosophy and Theology of Pantaleon Iroegbu.* Ibadan: Hope.

Wilson, B. (1983). *Religion in Sociological Perspective*. New York: Oxford University Press.

Wankar, G. T. (2015). "The One Who handed me over to you is Guilty of Greater Sin" (John 19:11): Examining the Violence of the Tiv/Fulani Crisis. *The Aquinas Journal*, Vol. 7, pp. 90-109.

CHAPTER TEN

THE PLACE OF AFRICA IN GLOBALIZATION

Peace I. Osaghae & Paul T. Haaga, Ph.D.

Executive Summary

The concept of globalization has a relative long history that has generated enormous interest and debate among contemporary scholars. Globalization as a concept is not new to the world; even though some scholars as it were are of the opinion that globalization is categorized into three major phases - 1870-1914, 1945-1980 and from 1980 till date. With regard to Africa, international contacts and exchanges are not new; hence, Africa's history is marked by foreign involvement. Africa has been in contact with other parts of the world and also had significant interactions within it. Interaction with the outside world particularly Europe and America started way back in the 15th century and this has significantly altered the course of Africa history- culturally, politically, economically and so on. This paper attempts a conceptual assessment of globalization; the paper examines the corollary of globalization and the place of Africa in a globalized world with the aim of establishing that what unifies us as humans in the global world is more fundamental than what differentiates us.

Keywords: Africa, Colonialism, Racism, Globalisation, Interdependence, Migration/Immigration

Introduction

There is no unanimous agreement about the inception of globalization although many are of the view that the phenomenon was quickened with the end of the multilateral division of the world occasioned by the dismantling of the Second World. However, authors like Karl Marx, Immanuel Wallerstein and Roland Robertson to mention a few, locate 1500 AD as the starting point of globalization. There are other scholars who share a different opinion about the inception of globalization. For instance, Anthony Giddens is of the view that modernity is the theme song of globalization and the 1800s marked its beginning. According to Tomlinson globalization began as recently as the 1960s with cultural planetization. Nevertheless, NederveenPieterse points out that these views imply that the history of modernity/globalization began with the history of the West and therefore these views are not only geographically narrow but also historically shallow (Pieterse, 1994). These speculations are pointers to the fact that there is no consensus about the advent of globalization.

However, it is essential to identify certain central tendencies associated with the process of globalization which started in the sixteenth century. In retrospect there exists different mode of globalization prior to 1500. For instance the anthropologist Eric Wolf's survey of the world in 1400 shows that there were well-formed civilizations in the Orient and the existence of states and polities in Africa as well as in the Americas. The significance of the remark should be seen against the widespread tendency in Europe to view colonialism as a civilizing mission and political anthropologists' assertion that pre-modern African polities were 'state-less.' Convinced that the Africans were incapable of self-rule, Europeans apportioned Africa at the Berlin Conference held in 1885 in the most haphazard vein, completely shattering the integrity of the 'nations' of Africa. Marx, Durkheim, and Weber, in spite of the fact that they were so different in their ideological orientations, have all contributed to marginalization of the 'nations' of Africa as well as others. Marx and Engels referred to the less developed nations as 'people without history,' 'remains of nations,' 'ruins of people' and their hope was to get attached to more 'progressive' nations, which were large,' 'well-defined,' 'historical,' and 'great'; who possessed 'undoubted vitality.' The notion of national self-determination by the people was inapplicable to Africans because being a people without history they are not nations in colonial Europe's perception. Having accepted the western anthropologists' certification that African Society is stateless the colonizers have set out to plant modern states in Africa. Relying on Weber's notion that the state is the only institution endowed with the authority to handle public violence, European colonizers appropriated the right to control the African people (Oomen, 2006). Colonialism is one central tendency associated with the process of globalization. In turn, a vital factor of colonialism is racism which implies the superiority of one group over another. Before now, the Eurasia race (i.e. Europe and Asia) caused a distortion in the African independence owing to the belief that Africans are less humans among other things. The Eurasia race was made up of the Caucasian race that tenaciously believes that they are superior to the Africans and this has had a negative toe on the African personality. Alex QuaisonSaiky- a Ghanaian defined Africa personality as a movement and the totality of an African world view. He tried to envisage Africa as it should be. The African personality entails the totality of the our world view and how we see ourselves, i.e. if you see yourself as inferior then that is what you are but if you see yourself otherwise (superior) and you have self esteem, it generates or redefine you as an African. This invariably makes up your personality. Our culture, race, norms and values are the things that count in defining the African personality. The average African is a human being and he has been denied this by other race, he gradually accepts it and this becomes his problem. Against this back drop, let us now proffer a clarification of the concept of globalization.

On the Conception of Globalization

In retrospect, the 'standard of civilization' in international society, a step towards globalization, was fixed by the West. These standards reflected the norms and values of the European civilization rooted in the mores of Christendom (Gong 1984:14–15). In other words the ideal of civilization which was imbedded in Christian conventions was determined by the West. The essential nature of globalization is the compression of space and time, so that people from distant areas are able and in fact obliged to interact with one another intensively and in a wide range of areas. As a result, the world becomes one, and interactions among diverse people begin to look like those within a village. Thus, the term "One World" is sometimes used as a synonym for globalization. In its contemporary form, globalization is driven by a variety of forces. These are financial or the flow of financial resources, economic with particular reference to the flow of goods and services and, to a very limited extent, labor, technology, especially transport, communications and information technology, the spread of culture from one corner of the world to the other, and the global diffusion of religious ideas as well as ideologies. According to Nsibambi (2001), Globalization is "a process of advancement and increase in interaction among the world's Countries and peoples facilitated by progressive technological changes in locomotion, Communication, political and military power, knowledge and skills, as well as interfacing of Cultural values, systems and practices". He noted that globalization is not a value-free, innocent, self-determining process. It is an international socio-politico-economic and cultural permeation process facilitated by policies of governments, private corporations, international agencies and civil society organizations. It essentially seeks to enhance and deploy economic, political, technological, ideological and military power and influence for competitive domination in the world. Globalization is a process that breaks down all barriers separating nations and continents with the aim of bringing mankind closer together (Daouas, 2000:1). According to Omoregbe (2007), it is a natural process of socialization hence; it is inevitable because it is part of human nature to socialize and interact with others. Man by nature is a social being with an irresistible urge to associate with his fellow human beings and globalization is a manifestation of this natural tendency in man. Globalisation refers to the integration of economic, political, social, cultural, technological, and environmental relations across international boundaries. It implies the opening of local and nationalistic perspectives to a broader outlook of an interconnected and interdependent world with free transfer of services across national frontiers, thereby ensuring that commonalities exist worldwide to make understanding, growth and development in the world map more attainable. Through the global interactions, cultures are fussing in several new dimensions, hence the multiculturalism that exists in the world today. Globalization has created a virtual village where actions taken in one part of the world system has almost instantaneous effects on other parts (Vaughan et.al, 2005). That is, the actions carried out in one society usually have consequences in other societies. Let us briefly look at various scholars' conception of globalization.

The Concept of Globalization and the African Experience

Over time, the general trend in the current debate on globalization revolves around the view that the phenomenon has negatively affected states from the underdeveloped parts of the world especially Africa. The argument of the scholars, especially those of the 'Critical School', is that globalization presents some countries with opportunities to develop, while other countries continue to witness widespread violence and poverty, and also to manifest symptoms of decadence as a result of globalization. This is what has been described as the paradox of globalization. Globalization as the basic defining element of the new world order, presents us with a paradox. The apparent integration of global cultures exists along with its anti-thesis: the prevalence of fragmentation in many areas of the same world (Offor, 2006).Economically, globalization has, on the whole, reinforced the economic marginalization of African economies and their dependence on a few primary goods for which demand and prices are externally determined. This has, in turn, accentuated poverty and economic inequality as well as the ability of the vast number of Africans to participate meaningfully in the social and political life of their countries. It has rendered the policies of nation-states governments and groups impotent to the extent that anti-citizenship policies are now pursued in the interest of a global world order to the detriment of the internal conditions of citizens within a country. This understanding of globalization can be seen in the activities of IMF and the World Bank in Nigeria where anti-citizenship policies with respect to education are being pursued.Other aspects that are unique to the present form of globalization are the Americanization of the world, the propagation of a universal paradigm for economic and political development, and the dominance of unilateralism as a way of conducting international relations. The Americanization of the World is the result of the huge and unprecedented gap between the United States and its nearest rival in each and every sphere, military, economic, technological and cultural, which is in turn transformed into the unequaled American influence on international issues and decision-making, including those within the purview of major international institutions such as the United Nations System, the Bretton-Woods institutions, and the World Trade Organization.Within this system, decisions and outcomes are largely the result of American unilateralism. A major consequence of this is the propagation of a universal paradigm for both economic and political development, in the form of the so-called Washington Consensus, whose main features are market forces and liberal democracy, without regard to the historical and cultural specificities of individual countries. In fact, globalization seems to be leading inexorably to the homogenization of the world, with the United States as the model and the standard by which all other countries are to be judged.

As a result of the cultural domination from outside that goes with globalization, African countries are rapidly losing their cultural identity and therefore their ability to interact with other cultures on an equal and autonomous basis, borrowing from other cultures only those aspects that meet its requirements and needs. In fact, it can lead to loss of cultural and national identity. It can lead to loss of one's individual identity which can result to inauthenticity. It can lead to a subtle form of neo-colonialism (Omoregbe, 2007).Globalization has therefore increasingly taken the appearance of the transformation of the international system from a multipolar or bipolar system to an imperial system under American hegemony. From the fore going, it is pertinent that we identify some of the merits and demerits as well as examine some natural consequence of globalization.

The Corollary of Globalization in Africa

Globalization as a phenomenon, however, has both positive and negative consequences. Here we shall be examining some of the merits and demerits of globalization among others. Underlying the views and arguments in support of globalization is the idea that it is a powerful engine of world prosperity which would bring about sustainable economic growth for all people of the world, particularly peoples of the Third World countries (Rogoff, 2003:10). He is of the view that globalization is an antidote to global inflation. It has some positive effects on African culture, for example, some inhuman cultural practices directed especially at women e.g. female genital mutilation (circumcision), widowhood rites, etc are being addressed and modified. This is a very significant positive impact of globalization on African culture. It opens people's lives to other cultures and all their creativity and to the flow of ideas and values, information and communication technologies have eased interaction among countries and peoples. That is, it facilitates contact with people in other parts of the world and brings people all over the world closer together (Kwame, 2011), it is necessary for the survival of mankind through interaction; it fosters mutual help, concern and understanding (Omoregbe, 2007).Then the demerits are that as cultures interact, some cultures are being diluted and or destroyed at the expense of others and negative values are being spread all over the world with relative ease. It has broaden the gap between the bourgeoisie and the proletariat, i.e., The world is now divided between the connected, who know and who have a monopoly on almost everything and the isolated, who do not know and who practically have nothing (Kwame, 2011). In order words, it has given more opportunities for the extremely wealthy to make money more quickly. These individuals have utilized the latest technology to move large sums of money around the globe extremely quickly and speculate ever more efficiently; i.e., it has further polarized the haves and the have not's. This is reflected in the neighbourhood in which they live and easy mobility for the affluent which make them ever so global while the poor are further localized with travel restrictions and controls (Omonzejele, 2004).

In addition to the fore going, another accompaniment of globalization is interdependence. This is a situation in which two or more entities simultaneously rely on one another for sustenance. Universally, interdependence involves mutual reliance and cooperation.Interdependence as it were has made it possible for globalization to thrive across international borders. Over the years, the human society has been characterized by varying degrees of interdependence. We depend on one another to accomplish both profound and mundane objectives (Payne, 2009). In other words, the human entity has been known to be interdependent for various reasons. For instance we import or export most of the food, drinks and drugs we consume; the clothes we wear, the cars we drive in and the materials with which we construct our infrastructures. Overall therefore, the negative consequences of globalization on Africa far outweigh their positive impact. To reverse this situation, Africa must meet two major challenges. The first is to introduce far- reaching changes in the assumptions, values and objectives of the existing states, so as to transform them into truly developmental states that are strong without being authoritarian. The second is to diversify African economies away from dependence on a few primary commodities, especially depleting natural resources which constitute enclaves in the overall economy, ensure a balance between agriculture and manufacturing, and increase the competitiveness of African goods in the world market. The achievement of these goals would require energetic and concerted action by governments, civil society, other stakeholders, and society at large, with active and sustained support from the international community. The enduring potential of the institution of the state is yet to be fully realized in the African continent due to lack of good governance resulting from bad leadership. The failure of most African states therefore, to face up to the challenges of globalization should not be blamed on globalization. What African states need to stir them aright in navigating the global terrain and reaping the gains of globalization is good governance, which can only be provided by good leadership. The quest for good governance and the search for good leaders; does not necessarily need to take Africans beyond the boundaries of their cultural values, as an abundance of virtues existed, in various traditional African societies, attributes that were promotive of good leadership and good governance. A proper exploration, appreciation and appropriation of such habits of virtue would go a long way in producing the right kind of governance that would enhance the capacity of states in Africa, to properly navigate the global terrain and reap the gains of globalization, just like their counterparts in other regions of the world (Offor, 2006).

Africans migrate from their motherland for much the same reasons that other immigrants do. Broadly categorized, these reasons include the economical, educational, social or political motivations that either push immigrants into leaving their countries of origin and settling in a new country, or those that pull them into seeking immigration to a given country. Push factors that stimulate migration from Africa include low pay, lack of employment, underemployment, poor educational system, absence of family members owing to prior migration and exposure to endemic violence, persecution and oppression. Pull factors include among other things; the possibility of earning a higher income, finding employment, better education, joining family members and hope for freedom from violence, persecution and oppression. Push factors usually create the desire to emigrate while pull factors provide the opportunity to act on that desire. Classified according to immigration status, one finds among Africans temporary migrants, permanent residents, naturalized citizens, exiles and refugees. Myron Weiner posits that global trends determine the pattern of migration. In his view, there are identifiable changes in the patterns of international migration which are linked to other international flows, including the movement of trade, capital, investment and information. The predominant cause of international migration is the change in the immigration policies of countries in response to global changes (Okome, 2005). This goes to show that the pursuit of globalization policies by some nation-states often leads to the increasing wave of migration in Africa countries to the countries of the West, all in the name of the search for greener pastures. The increasing number of interested applicants for the American visa lottery in Nigeria, for instance, is food for thought (Idowu, 2004). Also, economic and social stagnation has triggered a substantial brain- drain from Africa, further weakening the ability of African countries to manage their economies efficiently and effectively. Nothing beats the problems associated with globalization more than the capacity and the ability of any one nation to provide the enabling environment to generate and sustain opportunities for its citizens and indeed for all those who fall within its borders. African leaders should, therefore, put in place favourable working condition to prevent brain- drain. Having taken into consideration some of the consequences of globalization, we shall now have an insight into Africa's contact with the global world.

Africa and the Contact with the Global World

Africa is one of the continents in the world; and it is the second largest continent both in area and population, having an area of 11,699 square miles, more than three times the size of USA. In 1990, Africa had a population of 642 million representing 12% of the world's population. Africa is made up of over fifty nations with an estimated one thousand different languages spoken and as many distinct ethnic group. Africa is perhaps the most linguistically and ethnically diverse of the entire world's continent. Africa is endowed with immense natural and human resources, as well as great cultural, ecological and economic diversity. In terms of natural resources, Africa is the world's richest continent. It has 50% of world's gold, most of the world's diamonds and chromium, 90% of the cobalt, 40% of world's potential hydro-electric power, 65% of the manganese, millions of acres of untilled farmland and other natural resources such as crude oil and gas (Kwame, 2011). The land mark bordered by the Mediterranean Sea, Atlantic Ocean, Indian Ocean and the red sea is known as Africa.

Africa's contact with the rest of the world started through trade, including the trans-Atlantic slave trade. This was the period when western merchants bought from African slave traders Africa's most valuable resources (able-bodied men, women and children). The second was the era of colonialism, when Europeans at a conference in Berlin in 1884 divided up Africa among themselves and instituted direct control and rule over African countries. This division was done without regard to ethnic, cultural, linguistic and other considerations. The next stage of Africa's interaction with the world particularly Europe was during the era of independence from colonial rule. Beginning the last decade of the 20th century into the 21st century, Africa's linkage with other parts of the world has entered a new phase commonly termed as *globalization*. Though the term globalization may be new, the substance and ideals are not new to Africa and the world as a whole.

In spite of these impressive facts on Africa, for much of history and even in contemporary times most non-Africans have referred to it as the "Dark continent". In the past this reference was a reflection of the ignorance of the people of the west of Africa's immense potential. However in recent years, reference to Africa as the Dark Continent is mainly due to the over emphasis of negative reportage on Africa by the western media. Africa countries of course confront very real and severe challenges but not as the western media exaggerate. What the western media has failed to notice and to include in their reportage is that, in spite of the political, social and economic challenges confronting Africa, Africa is not in the throes of total disintegration and decay. Reports on African issues are most often ahistorical with no attempt to provide a historical context of antecedents of the issue. Many believe that most of the political and economic issues of contemporary Africa have deep seated roots in the colonial and post colonial experience i.e. effects of the cold war and globalization.

The capacity and reach of the African states, the absence of democratic structures and practice, the ethnic, civil and religious conflicts that have plagued post colonial Africa is a reflection of the legacy of colonialism. Reflection and debate on these questions have hardly commenced among policy makers, representatives of civil society groups and other stakeholders in the African continent. This puts Africa at a disadvantaged position in marshalling its energies and resources to deal effectively with the process of globalization (Kwame, 2011).As a result of these, there are divergent points of view about the phenomena and the question that comes to mind is, exactly what features does it refer to? Equally controversial are the specific forms taken by globalization, the forces driving it, and its consequences for the global system and for particular groups of countries. From the fore going, Africa's contact with the rest of the world became vivid with slave trade. Having seen Africa's contact with the global world, it is crucial that we examine the situation of Africa in a globalized world.

The Place of Africa in a Globalized World

Apparently, Africa is a disadvantaged participant in the globalization process. However, this has been blamed on factors such as colonialism and neo-colonialism and subsequently hinged the concept of globalization on imperialism. Notable in the global space is the fact that the dominant nations of the world have technological, commercial capital resources and socio-political dominance over the dependent countries of Africa. It is obvious that the developed countries set the rules in the world political economy structure that has been well planned and directed by transnational bodies. This advantage has essentially made it possible for dominant countries of the West to impose conditions of exploitation and extract part of the domestically produced surplus. It is clear that the place of Africa in the global economic order is that of a subservient economy. Africa occupies the position of a dependent economy whose objective is to serve European interests. Consequently, globalization as imperialism (i.e. the concept is seen as a form of dominance or the subordination of one country or continent over another in order to maintain a relationship of unequal exchange) has made Africa not only poorer, underdeveloped, dependent, but also an enslaved and plundered continent Scholars like Toyo, Ijomah and others are of the view that globalization represents a conscious affirmation of imperialism and by extension the universalization of European values and virtues under the pretensions of constructing world unity based on globalization. Remarkable in this ideological mindset is the reasoning that globalization signifies a new order of colonization, marginalization and the emasculation of the African continent (Igbafen, 2004). In other words, the implementation of globalization has further impoverished the dependent countries of Africa.

Wey and Osagie (1984) argue that given the positive impact of technology, it still fosteredthe next tool of enslavement by the West. The type of technology brought to Africa was one that kept Africa perpetually enslaved to the West.In the same vein, Odia (2004) argues that western society is capitalist oriented and technology employs capital intensive techniques. These techniques are imported to technologically backward countries like those in Africa to aggravate their problems. Accordingly, this introduced Western culture and values. Commenting on the unfairness of global capitalism generally, George Soros (2000) argues that; the global capitalist system has proved a very uneven playing field. The gap between the rich and the poor is getting wider. This is dangerous, because a system that does not offer some hope and benefit to the losers is liable to be disrupted by acts of desperation.

Igbafen (2004) posits that, African leaders have carried the twin global policy of globalization–free market liberalization and deregulation, farther than what should ordinarily be the case. For instance, in many African countries successive governments have pursued with vigor, in defiance of public opinion, the programmes of SAP, deregulation, liberalization, privatization and globalization such that the state, true to the underlying philosophy of neo-liberal economy, has become largely irrelevant to many Africans. Simply put, free-market liberalization in many African countries appears socially costly and more politically dangerous than had been imagined or portrayed.

More so, another factor that is responsible for Africa's disadvantaged position in the global world is the resolution of endless disputes and conflicts. Disputes and conflicts abound everywhere in the world. They do have a value in accentuating diversity and creating the minimum acceptable environment for growth within acceptable norms and relations. They also are the greatest source of instability and create conditions that impede development and growth. Africa is almost often synonymous with endless disputes and conflicts. This is unfortunate as African lives and properties have been destroyed and opportunities have been lost in the process. This could account for the continent's lack of participation in the global economy. The end result is that Africa has been left behind. It also means that, at all times Africa has to play catch-up with the rest of the world. Endless disputes and conflicts do not accentuate Africa's active role on the global stage and neither do they ensure that Africa reaps any of the benefits of globalization. Instead, the sale of small scale arms, violence against women and children and the attendant vulnerability of selected groups further increases the bad sides of globalization in the promotion of trafficking in people, forced labour and outright slavery of children (Kufuor, 2009).

However, this paper does not argue that Africa should disconnect herself from the global community because African nations like other nations of the world don't seem to have an option as to whether or not to globalize with the rest of the world and no nation can actually produce all the goods that she needs. This implies that there is a degree to which a nation can be said to be independent. So, Africa's interdependence on other nations of the world should not always place it in the backward position. Thus, the paper suggested ways by which this can be achieved. To achieve this objective, African countries must invest heavily in building, developing and maintaining their social capital, especially health and educational facilities that cater for the broad masses of the people rather than to tiny elite. For only by developing its human resources would African countries be in a position to take control over their destinies and be in a strong position to deal effectively with the outside world (Kwame, 2011). Similarly, Rodney opines that Africa's development is possible only on the basis of a radical break with the international capitalist system, which has been the principal agency of underdevelopment of Africa over the last five centuries.

He blamed Africa's economic retardation on the operation of the imperialist system owing to the fact that they depleted Africa's wealth there by making it impossible to foster the development of her resources (Rodney, 2009). He however envisioned and worked on the assumption that the new development of Africans and other dependent peoples of the "periphery" would require what he called "a radical break with the international capitalist system," a courageous challenge to the failing "center" of the current world order.

Oladipo (2008) opines that, to fight colonialism, this view of Africa by the colonialists had to be debunked. And one way of approaching this task was to provide several accounts of African beliefs, values and cultural practices which, in the opinion of the scholars concerned, showed that the African past was not one long night of savagery from which the first Europeans acting on God's behalf delivered them. Another reaction of African ethnocentrism was that of African nationalists who postulated a collective African identity, which, although different, was not in any way inferior to European identity. Some African scholars and philosophers actually believed that these reactions to European denigration of African peoples were inadequate, and this partly prompted the discussion on what should be the nature of African philosophy.

While the scientific and technological forces unleashed by globalization have facilitated to some extent access by Africans to advanced technology and information, this has been at the expense of stultifying the indigenous development of technology and distorting patterns of production in Africa, notably by utilizing capital as against labor intensive methods of production, which in turn increases unemployment and poverty. We must first understand that Africa is backward in terms of science and technology and in economic progress. This also explains its economic, political and military weakness; all of these have a bearing on its position at the bottom of the global hierarchy. African countries must therefore invest heavily in developing the scientific and technological skills and capabilities of its people. In this respect, national, sub-regional and regional institutions engaged in research and development should be established and strengthened, and close and active cooperation developed among them. Cooperation with scientific and technological institutions in the South, as well as with those in the developed world, should also be encouraged. At the level of international institutions, African countries must work energetically to change the rules and regulations, which limit their access to advanced technology, at a reasonable price, while frustrating their efforts at developing indigenous technologies (Kwame, 2011).

Therefore, a complete turnaround of our educational system is vital to our making a unique contribution to the globalization process. Education in pre-colonial Africa was relevant to Africa unlike what was introduced by the colonialists that has endured until date. We should re-introduce an educational system closely linked with social life and holistic in nature, a system, which does not separate theory from practice or learning from productivity, a system which does not select manual from the intellectual (Rodney, 1972:262). In other words, Africa should embark on the re-ordering of values, i.e., emphasis should be placed on the intellectual culture over the materialistic culture; and the need to develop a scientific culture which is crucial to human development within any nation.

According to Oladipo (1998:1), in an address delivered by Nyerere on the occasion of the convocation ceremony at the University of Ibadan in 1976, political independence has brought no change in economic conditions and very little social change. And unless Africa asserts its values, worldviews and paradigms of assessing reality in the globalization process, the problem of inequality will remain; and inequalities among states "both shape the process of globalization and are affected by it" (Hurrel and Wood, 1995). Africa must develop the capacity for self conscious change in our interaction with the global community. In developing its citizens, African countries should pay particular attention to strengthening their cultural identities. Culture should however be broadly defined and encompass not only attitudes, values, language, arts, music, dance, and other social mores and behavior, but should also include science and technology which play an important role in the development and spread of culture. This is one in which Africa is perhaps weakest, and explains the apparent fragility of African cultures in their encounter with other cultures. This does not mean that African countries should not learn and benefit from the cultures of other societies. All cultures are dynamic and undergo change, either through internal forces or by interaction with other cultures. Africa should do the same, but must make sure that it does not abandon its own culture in the process by mechanically aping and uncritically swallowing those of others. In this regard, African countries could learn from Japan and East Asian countries that have succeeded in strengthening their cultural identities by reinforcing their indigenous cultures while selectively adopting and adapting aspects of western culture that they find useful (Kwame, 2011).

Globalization and the interests in the African landscape, economic resources, environmental resources and manpower resources; are not positive but negative. The interest of the global world order is not in alleviating the crisis of development in Africa but in the exploitation of resources. For example, in Nigeria, the activities of the multinational corporations such as Shell and the Nigerian State in the Niger Delta area of Nigeria are a case in point. At the heart of the crisis in the Niger Delta is the struggle to realize the gains and privileges of citizenship in the face of the draconian policies pursued by the Nigerian State and its global partners (Idowu, 2004). Both the natural and human resources in Africa should be used efficiently to solve the numerous problems within the nations from where they are derived. By this we mean that the situation whereby natural resources are being exported to the western nations for foreign exchange at the expense of national development needs to be revamped. In addition, globalization seems to be leading inexorably to the homogenization of the world, with the United States as the model and the standard by which all other countries are to be judged. Notwithstanding, globalization is good but we must embrace it with caution and guard against the dangers inherent in it. Since Africa as a continent is poorer than the West, and since globalization is a Western concept, there is the need to tread gently in the process of globalization. This suggests the need for caution in Africa's involvement in the whole process (Odia, 2004).Globalization was not something that was planned or decided at a conference table by certain states or individuals. Rather it is a natural process of socialization, a process of world history, a phase in the world historical process. However, it can be controlled in such a way as to improve the economic conditions of developing countries. If developing countries are to benefit from globalization, there has to be a genuine intention and effort on the part of developed countries to help the developing countries, especially, to help their economies grow instead of worsening it (Omoregbe, 2007).

John A. Kufuor, former president of the Republic of Ghana; suggested that, given the general agreement on Africa's historical, psychological, political and economic handicaps which must be radically overcome, it is my belief that the continent needs the following critical tools to empower it to leap-frog into the mainstream of globalization: A leadership with a comprehensive grasp of, and knowledge of; (i) Africa's history, (ii) the economic dynamics of international relations, (iii) the development imperatives that Africa must employ to enhance its competitive advantages, rationally deployed on whatever comparative advantages are available, and ensuring that human capital development is central to those advantages, (iv) the necessity for vigorous provision of Education, Health Care, and Physical Infrastructure including Transportation, Energy, Telecommunications, Food Security, Potable Water and Environmental Balance in each and every nation, (v) awareness that healthy and vigorous symbiotic development of macro and micro-economies dictates public-private partnership policies as a cornerstone of socio-economic advancement, (vi) good governance issuing from constitutional imperatives of institutional checks and balances, respect for human rights as the basis for democracy; respect for minority rights, property rights, cultural and religious rights, transparent and accountable government and also responsible citizenship under law and order, with due process of the rule of law, (vii) appreciation of the decisive benefits of economies of scale from customs unions of regional groupings on the continent, including attracting FDI's for industrialization and job creation.

Conclusion

In conclusion, this paper posits that Africa should not disconnect herself from the global community because African nations like other nations of the world don't seem to have an option as to whether or not to globalize with the rest of the world and no nation can actually produce all the goods that she needs. We also suggested that African countries must invest heavily in building, developing and maintaining their social capital, especially health and educational facilities that cater for the broad masses of the people rather than to depend solely on other nations.

Also, from the fore going, it will not be out of place to identify colonialism as one central tendency associated with the process of globalization. In turn, a vital factor of colonialism is racism which implies the superiority of one group over another. The average African is a human being and he has been denied this by other race, he gradually accepts it and this becomes his problem. Human beings all over the world are unified by virtue of the fact that they share biological-cultural identity as homo-sapiens (Wiredu, 1996). As such, all humans are equal as we share in the same biological make-up. This status implies that we are organisms that go beyond instinct in the drive for equilibrium and self-preservation in specific ways, namely, by means of reflective perception, abstraction, deduction and induction. Reflective perception here means an awareness that involves the identification of objects and events through the conscious application of concepts which entails the power of recall and re-identification. Any being capable of reflective perception is already possessed of a concept of the external world. Human behavior is governed by both instinct and culture; because of the element of instinct, we can be sure of a certain species-distinctive uniformity in human actions and reactions and because of the element of culture, that is, of habit, instruction and conscious thought, there will naturally be plenty of room for variation. Naturally, being a human person implies having the capacity of reflective perception, abstraction and inference.

These mental capacities are the same for all humans, irrespective of whether they inhabit Europe, America, Asia or Africa. Particularly, the concept of object in general is the same for all beings capable of reflective perception. That is, there is a common human identity. The human constitution of flesh and bones quickened by electrical charges and wrapped up in variously pigmented integument, is the same everywhere; while there is only one world in which we all live, move and have our struggles, notwithstanding such things as the vagaries of climate. By this very fact, all human beings are kindred (Wiredu: 1996). In this respect, article one of the universal declaration of human rights states that, "all human beings are born free and equal in dignity and rights. They are endowed with reason and conscience and should act towards one another in a spirit of brotherhood" (UDHR).   Some of the reasons why Africa is believed to have always been at a disadvantaged position are that; we blame all our problems on colonialism, we have not actually concentrated our efforts to solving the problems of backwardness in a fast growing global society, Africa has always been a consumptions oriented society rather than a producing society and Africa has come to accept that western paradigm must be used to judge development in Africa. Nevertheless, Africa has been globalizing through its interactions with the rest of the world.

References

Article 1 *UDHR*.The United Nations Department of Public Information. Nov 2007.

Daouas M. 2001. "Africa Faces Challenges of Globalization" in *Finance and Development*, International Monetary Fund, Vol.38, No.4, December (website edition).

Hurrel A. and Wood N. 1995. "Globalisation and Inequality", in *Journal of International Studies*, Vol.24, No.3, Winter.

Gong G. W. 1984. *The Standard of 'Civilization' in International Society*. Oxford: Clarendon Press.pp.

Idowu, W. 2004. "Globalization, Citizenship and the African Predicament" in *Philosophy and Praxis in Africa*. M.F. Asiegbu and J.C.A. Agbakoba. Ed. Ibadan: Hope Publications. pp.269-276.

Igbafen M.L. 2004."Africa in a Globalised World", in *Philosophy and Praxis in Africa*.M.F. Asiegbu and J.C.A. Agbakoba. Ed. Ibadan: Hope Publications. pp. 287-300

Kufuor, J.A. 2009. A Statement at the International Conference on Africa and Globalisation: Learning from the Past, Enabling a Future, 28-29 September, Tokyo, Japan.

Kwame, Y. 2011. "The Impact of Globalization on African Culture".Retrieved online at www.africanresource.com on November 9, 2011.

Mojubaolu O. O. 2005. "Globalization and Marginalization", in *The Antinomies of Globalization*.O.Vaughan, M. Wright and C. Small. Ed. Ibadan: Sefer Books Ltd. p. 92

Nsibambi A. 2001. "The Effects of Globalization on the State in Africa: Harnessing the benefits and minimizing the costs". Paper presented at UN General Assembly, second committee: Panel discussion on globalization and the state, November 2, 2001.

Odia S.I. 2004. "Globalization and African Philosophy", in *Philosophy and Praxis in Africa*. M.F. Asiegbu and J.C.A. Agbakoba. Ed. Ibadan: Hope Publications. pp. 277-286.

Offor F. 2006. "Globalisation and State Collapse in Africa: A Critique of the Critical Theorist Perspective", in *Journal of Social Development in Africa*.Vol. 21.No.2. pp.11-30.

Oladipo O. 2008. *Thinking about Philosophy: A General Study Guide*. (Ibadan: Hope Publications) p. 64.

Omonzejele P.F. Alienation in a Globalised World.*Philosophy and Praxis in Africa*.M.F. Asiegbu and J.C.A. Agbakoba. Ed. Ibadan: Hope Publications. pp.301-308.

Omoregbe J.I. 2007.*Social-Political Philosophy and International Relations: A Systematic and Historical Study*. Vol. 1 (Lagos: Joja Educational Research and Publishers Ltd). pp. 155- 156.

Oommen T.K. 2006. "On the Historicity of Globalization: Construction and Deconstruction of "Others" in *Social Change in the Age of Globalization*. J. Tiankui et.al. Ed. Boston: Brill Leiden. pp. 3-17.

Payne R.J. 2009. *Global Issues: Politics, Economics and Culture* -2[nd]ed. (New York: Pearson Education, Inc.) p.14.

NederveenPieterse, J. P. 1994. "Globalization as Hybridization."*International Sociology*, 9(2), 161–84.

Rodney W. 2009.*How Europe Underdeveloped Africa*.(Pretoria: Panaf Publishing) xii & xiii.

Rogoff K.S. "Disinflation: An Unsung Benefit of Globalization" *Finance and Development*, a publication of IMF. Washington: December 2003.

Soros G. 2000. *Open Society: Reforming Global Capitalism*. (Great Britain: Little Brown and Company) xix.

"The Challenges of Globalization in Africa: What Role for Civil Society and Other Stakeholders?"Paper presented at UN General Assembly in Addis Ababa Ethiopia. November 4, 2002.

UNESCO, International Conference: Africa and Globalisation: Learning from the Past, Enabling a Better Future. 28-29 September 2009, Tokyo, Japan.

Uroh C.O."Globalisation and the Question of Gender Justification: The Nigerian Experience".A paper delivered at CODERSIA Conference, available at http/www.codersia.org/links/ conferences/uroh.

Wey S.O. and Osagie E. 1984.*The World at Adult Stage*.Ibadan: Evans Brothers Ltd.

Wiredu K. 1996. *Cultural Universals and Particulars: An African Perspective*. (Indiana Polis: Indiana University Press) 22 & 23

CHAPTER ELEVEN

FANON'S THEORY OF VIOLENCE AND ITS RELEVANCE TO CONTEMPORARY VIOLENCE IN AFRICA

Aghamelu, Fidelis Chuka & Ejike, Emeka Cyril

Executive Summary

The main thrust of this paper is to demonstrate that Fanon's thesis of violence is relevant to violence in modern times. It explores Fanon's analysis of colonial violence and violence for liberation. It then argues that socio-economic deprivation and alienation which he identifies as the root causes of racial and tribal violence in the colonial world are responsible for the outbreak and escalation of racial and ethnic violence in modern society, especially Africa. Rather than subscribe to Fanon's belief in revolution, this paper recommends that restructuring of socio-political systems, and development of humans and infrastructure, among others, remain major panaceas for contemporary violence in Africa.

Keywords: Colonialism, Violence, Decolonization, Freedom.

Introduction

Like every other philosopher, Fanon is a child of his time. His time, his world and existence is the colonial world – a Manichean world. He wrote from this specific time and history. It is therefore necessary to furnish ourselves, by way of introduction, with circumstances and events in the colonial world which shaped his life and thoughts. Fanon was born on 20th July, 1925 on the Island of Martinique. He was one of the descendants of slaves shipped to the Island in the 17th century. It was a society in which economic condition and social status mainly depended on colour. In Martinique blacks were subjected to French education aimed at assimilating them into French culture and language. However, the French policy of assimilation, in Fanon's case, was countered by the influence of Aime Césaire who was propounding the philosophy of negritude as an intellectual reaction to alienated consciousness experienced by the black people as well as an affirmation of their existence and culture.

So, while the influence of French education was moving the young Fanon towards assimilation, Césaire's negritude was tilting him towards self autonomy. He was therefore "plagued during much of his life by the demands of assimilation and the need for autonomy, the need to be one's authentic self. He embodied within himself these two contradictory positions."[1] The outbreak of Second World War interrupted Fanon's education and he was enlisted in the Free French Army to fight for the French. His travels during war brought him face-to-face with the experience of racism in Europe, Africa and in the French Caribbean. He observed that in the army France had a different place for Black Frenchmen despite the value of liberty, equality and fraternity it proclaims.

Fanon returned to school to complete his education when the war ended. At this time, his teachers observed that he became more and more withdrawn and introspective, suggesting that he was going over his war experience in his mind. He then turned his attention to the work of philosophers such as Jean Paul Satre, Aime Césaire, Karl Jaspers, Soren KierKegaard and Friedrich Nietzsche. In 1847 Fanon went to France to study Medicine with a specialization in Psychiatry at the University of Lyon. During his medical training he continued to study the works of philosophers, including Karl Marx, Martin Heidegger, Edmund Husserl and Friedrich Hegel. After completing his studies, we went to Algeria in 1953 to serve as head of the Psychiatry department of Blida-Joinville Hospital in Algeria. In the hospital Fanon began to observe the effects of colonial violence on the human psyche, as he was giving Algerians and French soldiers treatment.

Fanon's study and experience of the existential conditions of the oppressed people in France and Algeria prompted him to join National Liberation Front (FLN) and work actively for Algeria's liberation. By day he would work for the French administration, while by night he would work for the Algerian nationalists. When it dawned on him that he could no longer cope with this double role, he resigned from the psychiatric job to devote himself wholeheartedly to the FLN and the Algerian revolution. He pointed out the futility of practising psychiatry in a degrading and dehumanizing colonial world in his letter of resignation. As he states it: "if psychiatry is the medical technique that aims to enable man no longer to be a stranger to his environment, I owe it to myself to affirm that the Arab, permanently an alien in his own country, lives in a state of absolute depersonalization."[2]

Fanon's war experiences and the legacy of colonial domination, together with his study of philosophical works and training as a psychiatrist, had a strong influence on his conception of decolonization within the context of anti-colonial struggle. It was the dehumanizing and excruciating circumstances in the colonial world that influenced Fanon's advocacy of revolutionary decolonization aimed at destroying the unjust colonial structures and liberating alienated consciousness.

Nature of Violence

Violence is the "use of force to harm or destroy human beings or non-human objects, for the purpose of preserving or altering political institutions, systems, governments, or policies."[3] Violence may be physical or psychological. Roberts explains that violence "contains dimensions of physical and psychological domination by one species of mankind over another."[4] Physical violence is the infliction or threat of infliction of painful injury by the use of instruments like whips, guns, bayonets and fists. Psychological violence involves the use of hostile behaviour such as gestures and words to cause emotional damage or harm to the victim. Both forms of violence are aimed at diminishing the victim's sense of identity, dignity and self-worth.

There are two distinct concepts of violence, namely instrumental violence and intrinsic violence. Instrumental violence refers to "a concept in which the implementation of either wanton irrational or calculated rational violence occurs as a means to an end."[5] This means that violence is employed with the sole purpose of achieving a specific result. Here, the party does not place a metaphysical value on the violent act but sees it merely as an instrumental means to attain an end. Intrinsic violence, in contrast to instrumental violence, refers to "a metaphysical concept in which the act of either random irrational or calculated rational violence itself contains inherent value."[6] Intrinsic violence does not operate in a means-end continuum; it places positive value on a violent act, regardless of the outcome at a specific moment of implementation.

Fanon conceives of violence in the colonial world as both physical and psychological. For him, violence is an intrinsic nature of the colonial system which produces alienated consciousness and alienating material conditions that are formidable obstacles to man's liberation. In response to colonial oppression and exploitation, Fanon believes that violence is intrinsically valuable in the anti-colonial struggle for freedom and therefore urges the decolonizing natives to extricate themselves from the grips of colonial domination and achieve equal status with the settlers by means of violence.

Fanon's Analysis of the Colonial Situation

Fanon notes that colonialism is violent in its natural state. In other words, he sees violence as the defining characteristic of colonialism. For him, colonial world is characterized by dichotomy between the settlers and the natives. It is deeply rooted in Manichean structure, that is, it is arranged in such a way that there is conflict or opposition between the settlers and the natives. Fanon states that colonial world is divided into two compartmental zones: the zone of the settlers and the zone of the natives. Barrack and police stations partition these zones. Narcissism and Chauvinism permeate the consciousness of the settlers. They see their zone as being the sole sphere of humanity. So, if one does not belong to that sphere, one cannot claim to represent a civilized human species.

The natives are being exploited, enslaved, oppressed, marginalized, dehumanized, abused and devalued by the colonizers. Fanon therefore writes: "The Negro problem does not resolve itself into the problem of Negroes living among white men but rather of Negroes exploited, enslaved, despised by a colonialist, capitalist society that is only accidentally white."[7] Fanon views colonialism as a system of exploitation which makes the colonized people feel inferior to the colonizers. He contends that the instrument of colonial rule is violence. This violence is cruelly executed by means of bayonets and canons and sustained by the police and the army. Fanon writes thus: "their first encounter was marked by violence and their existence together – that is to say the exploitation of the native by the settler – was carried on by dint of a great array of bayonets and cannons."[8] He explains further that in the colonial world:

> The policeman and the soldier, by their immediate presence and their frequent direct action maintain contact with the native and advise him by means of rifle butts and napalm not to budge. It is obvious here that the agents of government speak the language of pure force. The intermediary does not lighten the oppression, nor seek to hide the domination; he shows them up and puts them into practice with the clear conscience of an upholder of the peace; yet he is the bringer of violence into the home and into the mind of the native.[9]

The racially motivated physical violence is perpetrated to subject the natives to awful abuse and traumatic experience in order to force them into submission. In the light of this, Hansen explains that physical violence does not only refer to "the wars of conquest, pillage and plunder by which in many places colonial rule was established but also refer to the day employment of strong arm measures to keep the colonized population in a subject state."[10]

Psychologically, the colonized people are robbed of their being and made to feel inferior and worthless. To be human is to be white. The white is civilized and rational but the Negro is primitive, uncivilized and inhuman. The colonizers do not recognized the colonized people as being human and thus treats them inhumanely. Satre notes the physiological and psychological violence in the colonial world:

> Sheer physical fatique will stupefy them. Starved and ill, if they have any spirit left, fear will finish the job; guns are levelled at the peasant; civilians come to take over his land and force him by dint of flogging to fill the land for them. If he shows fight, the soldiers fire and he's a dead man; if he gives in, he degrades himself and he is no longer a man at all; shame and fear will split up his character and make his inmost self fall to pieces. The business is conducted with flying colors and by experts; the "psychological services" weren't established yesterday; nor was brainwashing.[11]

Culturally, the natives are degraded and devastated colonialism robs the African culture of its essential value. The colonists present their culture as being superior to that of African and so the natives are made to view realities from the perspective of French culture. African culture which is once open to the future automatically becomes "closed, fixed in the colonial status, caught in the yoke of oppression."[12] In this way, African culture loses its autonomy and becomes an instrument of colonial oppression. Satre reveals that "violence in the colonies does not only have for its aim the keeping of these enslaved men at arm's length; it seeks to dehumanize them. Everything will be done to wipe out their traditions, to substitute our language for theirs and to destroy their culture without giving them ours."[13] Through the exploitative racism inherent in colonial rule the cultural legacy of the natives are destroyed and they are made to feel that their culture and all aspects of their being are inferior. As Kebede puts it: "The tag of primitiveness affixed on them, the contempt for and complete destruction of their cultural legacy, their forced assimilation into the European culture at a reduced price, all have resulted in the inculcation, deep into the soul of each colonized person, of a devastating inferiority complex."[14]

Structurally, colonialism creates economic alienation and alienated consciousness through exploitation that permeates into colonial, political and socio-economic structures. The natives are prohibited from participating meaningfully in the political processes which affect them and thus could not express their authentic existence. Though they are indispensable force, they are separated from their products. Through violence they are subjected to forced labour and made to think that their blackness bars them from possessing wealth and occupying high social status. Like Marx, Fanon holds that economic condition is the substructure of the colonial world which determines the superstructure. However, he identifies this substructure with the race so that material possessions and social status are tied to one's race. He asserts thus:

> When you examine at close quarters the colonial context, it is evident that what parcels out the world is to begin with the fact of belonging to or not belonging to a give race, a given species. In the colonies the economic substructure is also a superstructure. The cause is the consequence: you are rich because you are white, you are white because you are rich. This is why Marxist analysis should always be slightly stretched every time we have to do with the colonial problem.[15]

The above quote suggests that "the white man is the symbol of capital as the Negro is that of labor."[16] The implication of this is that the colonized people would remain impoverished, thereby leading to alienated consciousness and alienating material conditions.

This dehumanizing treatment of the natives and the Manichaeism of colonies generate conflicting demands, interests and identity. The colonists are desirous of privileges, domination and racial superiority, while the essential needs of the colonized people are land, communality, dignity and cultural expressions. The colonists consider themselves superior to the natives, while the natives refuse to accept their inhuman condition. In the light of this, Satre writes:

> Hatred, blind hatred which is as yet an abstraction, is their only wealth, the master calls it forth because he seeks to reduce them to animals, but he fails to break it down because his interests stop him halfway. Thus, the 'half-natives' are still humans, through the power and weakness of the oppressor which is transformed within them into a stubborn refusal of the animal condition.[17]

However, the natives are deprived of expressing their aggression. Though they are burning with rage, they dare not confront the well-armed colonists due to the psychological inhibitions created by the repressive colonial regime and the trepidation of being sanctioned. Consequently, colonial rule sets one native against the other. Initially, the colonized man applied defence mechanism. He "will manifest this aggressiveness which has been deposited in his bones against his own people"[18] as a way of relieving the emotional stress and avoiding violent confrontation with the colonizers. As Fanon puts it: "The settler keeps alive in the native an anger which he deprives of outlet; the native is trapped in the tight links of the chains of colonialism … The native's muscular tension finds outlet regularly in bloodthirsty explosions – in tribal warfare, in feuds between sects and, in quarrels between individuals."[19] Satre argues that the natives deteriorate their degrading and dehumanizing experience by transferring their repressed anger to one another. For him, such act does not amount to liberation but promotion of dehumanization. He explicates thus:

> At first it is not their violence, it is ours, which turns back on itself and rends them; and the first action of these oppressed creatures is to bury deep down that hidden anger which their and our moralities condemn and which is how ever only the last refuge of their humanity … If this suppressed fury fails to find an outlet, it turns in a vacuum and devastates the oppressed creatures themselves since they cannot face the real enemy … They can only stop themselves from marching against the machine-guns by doing our work for us; of their own accord they will speed up the dehumanization that they reject.[20]

In the light of this background, Fanon believes that tribal violence does not predate colonialism. He views both "tribal and social divisions as the conjuring of colonialism."[21] Violence, for him, emanates from colonialism which breeds and preserves tribal antagonism. Colonialism by its very structure is separatist and regionalist. Colonialism does not simply state the existence of tribes; it also reinforces and separates them …[22] On the part of nationalist bourgeoisie or political leaders, they manage their aggressiveness by assimilating themselves into the colonial system to such a degree that their interests are bound up with the interests of the colonizers. In the words of Fanon: "The native intellectual has clothed his aggressiveness in his barely veiled desire to assimilate himself to the colonial world. He has used his aggressiveness to serve his own individual interests."[23] Fanon explains that the nationalist bourgeoisie have no option but to conform to colonial model, having seen that the colonialist bourgeoisie have administrative apparatus in place to sanction and suppress dissenting and critical voices. The nationalist bourgeoisie are not part of the productive forces. Their duty is to ensure that colonial administration runs smoothly and effectively. They will seek some sort of compromise when the masses become increasingly restive, all in a bid to maintain the status quo and propagate the interests of the colonists as well as their own interests.

Fanon frowns upon reactionary attitudes of the nationalist bourgeoisie. He notes that they are complicit in the colonial domination and capitalist exploitation. For him, the nationalist political leaders allow themselves to be brainwashed and incorporated into the capitalists' and colonialists' desire for a peaceful settlement. They deny the violence and careless brutality structurally present in the colonial regime. They use anti-colonial struggle to acquire more power and serve their individual interests at the expense of the poor natives. Fanon argues that the nationalist bourgeoisie have taken for themselves the power and advantages that are heritage of the colonial era and have just replaced the colonist bourgeoisie. Having been assimilated into and aligned with the colonial system, they believe in the reformation agenda, rather than revolutionary violence. Although they are violent in their words before the common natives to keep the nationalist zeal alive, they are reformist in their attitudes. In other words, they speak a lot and in great words to their people without any action. They claim to be identifying with the plight of the poor natives, but they do not want the transformation of the colonial system. Fanon expresses the complicity of the nationalist bourgeoisie with the colonial regime and their betrayal of his people in this way:

> The entire action of these nationalist political parties during the colonial period is action of the electoral type: a string of philosophicopolitical dissertations on the themes of the rights of peoples to self-determination, the rights of man to freedom from hunger and human dignity, and the unceasing affirmation of the principle: "one man, one vote." The national political parties never lay stress upon the necessity of a trial of armed strength, for the good reason that their objective is not the radical overthrowing of the system. Pacifists and legalists, they are in fact partisans of order, the new order – but to the colonialist bourgeoisie they put bluntly enough the demand which to them is the main one: "Give us more power." On the specific question of violence, the elite are ambiguous. They are violent in their words and reformist in their attitudes. When the nationalist political leaders say something, they make quite clear that they do not really *think* it.[24]

This renewed aggression continues until violence against other natives changes direction. The aggression becomes unbearable to such an extent that the natives react to the colonizers' violence with their own violence. At this time, colonial violence only serves to provoke the natives' aggression against the settlers. Exploitative and oppressive colonial regime increases the consciousness that "between oppressors and oppressed everything can be solved by force."[25] The colonized people now identify their real foes as the colonists and come to believe that only violence can free them. They thus channel their violence towards the annihilation of the unjust colonial system. Fanon thus explains: "yet in spite of the metamorphoses which the colonial regime imposes upon it in the way of tribal or regional quarrels, that violence makes its way forward, and the native identifies his enemy and recognizes all his misfortunes, throwing all the exacerbated might of his hate and anger into this new channel."[26] However, the nationalist political leaders would not call for armed insurrection. Instead, they would opt for dialogue with the colonialist bourgeoisie in order to relax the tension and restore order. Fanon believes that all repressive measures and actions of the native elite cannot end colonial oppression. He sees any attempt by the natives to entrust their eventual freedom to negotiation between the native political elite and the colonizers as a false path. This is because, for him, the exploitative and oppressive rules will continue even if the colonial system is reformed so that the corrupt nationalist political elite rule the people directly under the dictates of the colonialist bourgeoisie.

In Fanon's view, arbitrary violence is an intrinsic quality of colonial system and so colonial government is a living negation of its proclaimed values. Hence, he writes: "when I search for man in the technique and the style of Europe, I see only a succession of negations of man and an avalanche of murders."[27] Given that the colonizers deny the humanity of the colonized people,

Fanon believes that it is a futile effort to persuade the colonizers to end colonial oppression for the sake of the humanity of the natives. For him, colonialism is an embodiment of injustice and so deserves to be destroyed by whatever means possible. The injustice of colonialism includes the suppression of people's right to self-determination, economic and racial exploitation, and violation of other democratic rights. Violent change would correct the injustice. The end of colonial exploitation would inaugurate "the unconditional reign of justice."[28] Fanon therefore thinks that the colonized peoples could "create the whole man, whom Europe has been incapable of bringing to triumphant birth"[29] through revolutionary violence.

Fanon's Decolonization/Revolutionary Theory of Violence

Fanon advocates violent revolution within the context of anti-colonial struggle. He contends that the absolute necessity of violent revolution stems from the violent nature of colonial world. Colonialism "is violence in its natural state, and it will only yield when confronted with greater violence."[30] Violence is a necessary ingredient of liberation without which there is no genuine freedom. He sees this violent break with colonialism as true decolonization that can only guarantee authentic liberation. In the light of this, Fanon writes: "National liberation, national renaissance, the restoration of nationhood to the people, commonwealth: whatever may be the headings used or the new formulas introduced, decolonization is always a violent phenomenon."[31] He explains that decolonization is a violent phenomenon because it is "the meeting of two forces, opposed to each other by their very nature, which in fact owe their originality to that sort of substantiation which results from and is nourished by the situation in the colonies."[32] Therefore, the Manichaeism inherent in the colonial system is preserved in the process of decolonization. This means that "the settler never ceases to be the enemy, the opponent, the foe that must be overthrown."[33]

Fanon shared the same view with Satre that the dialectic is the practical consciousness of an oppressed class struggling against its oppression."[34] This dialectic can only be resolved through "the dialectical reciprocity of antagonism."[35] As Fanon puts it: "The violence of the colonial regime and the counter-violence of the colonized balance each other and respond to each other in an extraordinary reciprocal homogeneity."[36] Decolonization, for him, is necessary violent because it seeks to right a situation that is created by violence in the colonial world. Just as colonization seeks to violently uproot the colonized people from their cultural placing and make them inhuman, so is decolonization a veritable means of creating new persons, so that natives become human during the same process by which they free themselves. Fanon argues thus:

> Decolonization never takes place unnoticed, for it influences individuals and modifies them fundamentally. It transforms spectators crushed with their inessentiality into privileged actors, with the grandiose glare of history's floodlights upon them. It brings a natural rhythm into existence, introduced by new men, and with it a new language and a new humanity. Decolonization is the veritable creation of new men ... the "thing" which has been colonized becomes man during the same process by which it frees itself.[37]

In Fanon view, therefore, it is only through violence that man creates himself. Violence restores the humanity of the colonized man which has been eroded by colonial violence. He contends further that:

> Irrepressible violence is neither sound nor fury, nor the resurrection of savage instincts, nor even the effect of resentment: it is man recreating himself ... no gentleness can efface the marks of violence; only violence itself can destroy them. The native cures himself of colonial neurosis by thrusting out the settler through force of arms. When this rage boils over, he rediscovers his lost innocence and he comes to know himself in that he himself creates his self. Far removed from this war, we consider it as a triumph of barbarism; but of its own volition it achieves, slowly but surely, the emancipation of the rebel, for bit by bit it destroys in him and around him the colonial gloom.[38]

He insists that the only true liberation is the liberation of the self from the self, that is, the liberation from a desire to become something other than the true self. In this case, it is the liberation from a desire by the blacks to become the whites. Thus, violence within the context of anti-colonial struggle becomes the necessary means of bringing the colonized person from a situation of alienation to the discovery of true self. For Fashina, anti-colonial violence is justified when it is directed towards a reclaim of the humanity of persons to whom this has been denied. So, "in order to win genuine respect, dignity, the colonized must force the settler's recognition through physical violence."[39] The colonized man reclaims his humanity by denying strenuously and completely all values that characterize the settlers, for the "Manicheism of the settler produces the Manicheism of the native."[40]

Again, Fanon claims that violence has a beneficial effect on the natives' psyche. For him, it has cathartic element or cleansing force which purges the natives' soul of ill psychological feelings accumulated as a result of the evil of colonialism which includes oppression, police brutality, racial discrimination and psychological abuses. In the words of Fanon: "At the individual level, violence is a cleansing force. It frees the native from his inferiority complex and from his despair and inaction; it makes him fearless and restores his self-respect."[41] The native man achieves psychological liberation and is rid of his inferiority complex when his oppressors are removed violently and the existing political and socio-economic structures are violently changed. Fanon notes, as stated before, that the colonial world is a white-dominated world. It is white to the extent that the colonized people internalize the racist standards of the colonizers and begin to fight against themselves. He now urges "black men to overcome their inferiority complexes by killing the white man within themselves."[42] But this is only possible through violence, for it is "the intuition of the colonized masses that their liberation must, and can only, be achieved by force."[43] Since anti-colonial violence is a redirection against the "perpetrators of the violence of colonialism itself,"[44] it will liberate the colonized people from inferiority complex and bring back "their lost self-respect, courage and their sense of self-worth."[45]

Fanon's contention is that the settlers first flout the universalized norms of conduct by denying the natives equal right to human dignity and respect and relegating them to the state of inhuman.

Thus, his concern is not about showing compliance with the universal norms, but to repel the oppressor through violence as a cathartic liberation of the soul. In this regard, he argues that "as far the native is concerned, morality is very concrete; it is to silence the settler's defiance, to break his flaunting violence – in a word, to put him out of the picture. The well-known principle that all men are equal will be illustrated in the colonies from the moment that the native claims he is equal of the settler."[46] Fanon therefore believes that the right thing to do is to employ violence to free the natives from their dehumanizing experience and restore their human dignity, identity and self-worth.

Besides, Fanon thinks violence for freedom unifies the people on a national basis and builds solidarity among them. He explains that violent struggle would re-unite the native intellectuals with his people and the intellectuals would abandon individualist principles which the colonialist bourgeoisie have made them embrace and then imbibe their rich and cherished traditional values. He explicates thus:

> The native intellectual had learnt from his masters that the individual ought to express himself fully, the colonialist bourgeoisie had hammered into the native's mind the idea of a society of individuals where each person shuts himself up in his own subjectivity, and whose only wealth is individual thought. Now the native who has the opportunity to return to the people during the struggle for freedom will discover the falseness of this theory ... such a colonized intellectual, dusted over by colonial culture, will in the same way discover the substance of village assemblies, the cohesion of people's committees, and the extraordinary fruitfulness of local meetings and groupments. Henceforward, the interests of one will be the interests of all. ...[47]

He explains further the alleged sociological function of revolutionary violence by claiming that it binds the colonized people together and mobilizes them to pursue their common cause and collective destiny. In the words of Fanon:

> The practice of violence binds them together as a whole, since each individual forms a violent link in the great chain, a part of the great organism of violence which has surged upward in reaction to the settler's violence in the beginning. The groups recognize each other and the future nation is already indivisible. The armed struggle mobilizes the people, that is to say, it throws them in one way and in one direction.[48]

In Fanon's view, therefore, the armed struggle builds solidarity among the natives and introduces into their consciousness "the ideas of a common cause, of a national destiny and of collective history."[49] For Fanon, when the masses are partakers of a violent struggle towards their national liberation, their confidence is built up and political consciousness is raised. They come to realise that their liberation is an outcome of their concerted efforts and not a one-man band. In this case, no one solely claims to be a liberator or has a special merit of national liberation. They now have a strong sense of destiny and dare not place their future "in the hands of a living god."[50] Thus, there is little or no room "for the rise and growth of the demagogues and the opportunists."[51]

Fanon insists that only revolutionary violence can liberate man's consciousness and create a new man, for "the colonized man finds his freedom in and through violence."[52] He thinks that all attempts to elucidate African history and juxtaposes it with European history are only the corollary of a profound inferiority complex. For instance, he argues that an attempt to study African past and romanticize it through negritude movement cannot solve the African problems and so is futile. He acknowledges the negritude, which Senghor characterizes as "the awareness, defense and development of African cultural values,"[53] for raising the consciousness of the blacks and affirming their cultural roots and values of civilization. However, Fanon agrees with Satre that negritude is an anti-white racism which merely negates white supremacy without effective strategy for black liberation. He expresses growing discontent with the idea of watching history unfold itself without any action. He asserts thus: "In no way should I dedicate myself to the revival of an unjustly unrecognized Negro civilization."[54] He states further in this regard:

> I am not a prisoner of history ... the real leap consists in introducing invention into existence. In the world through which travel, I am endlessly creating myself ... I am convinced that it would be of the greatest interest to be able to have contact with a Negro literature or architecture of the third century before Christ. I should be very happy to know that a correspondence had flourished between some Negro philosopher and Plato. But I can absolutely not see how this fact would change anything in the lives of the eight-year-old children who labor in the cane fields of Martinque or Guadeloupe.[55]

What Fanon is driving at is that consciousness cannot change reality. It must be backed up with a violent struggle to achieve freedom from colonial domination.

In a similar vein, Fanon follows Marx in maintaining that thought must be united with action. Like Marx, he insists that all that matters is not to know the world but change it. He writes thus: "But when one has taken cognizance of this situation, when one has understood it, one considers the job completed. How can one then be deaf for that voice rolling down the stages of history: 'What matters is not to know the world but to change it.' "[56] So, Fanon's advocacy of revolutionary violence in resistance to and defeat of oppression is in line with the Marxist revolutionary tradition. He notes that the nationalist bourgeoisie and the urban working class are reluctant to embark on a revolutionary violent against the system that benefits them enormously. They cannot perform this revolutionary role because they are "not only conditioned to operate in the colonial mode of production"[57] but have also "been subjected to colonial socialization"[58] which makes them accept such order as natural. Hansen asserts that it is not surprising that "a group which owes it entire privileged existence to such a system will not play a prime role in its abolition."[59]

Therefore, Fanon assigns the revolutionary role to the peasantry and lumpen-proletariat. Unlike the nationalist bourgeoisie and the urban working class, the peasantry are not integrated into the colonial system. They benefit nothing from colonial rule and are not corrupted by it. Fanon believes that the peasants are in touch with their culture and have not suffered from inferiority complex and cultural degradation. They are therefore potential revolutionaries who possess a great deal of brute force. Lumpen proletariat are also suitable for revolutionary violent. They consist predominantly of the unemployed and unemployable masses, a horde of starved men who have drifted from the countryside to the city but have not secured a place in the social system. They are willing to employ whatever means possible to achieve their ends. Fanon thinks that they have the proclivity to engage in an armed struggle against the colonial regime since they have no stake in the colonial system.

Relevance of Fanon's Thesis to Contemporary Violence

The fact that African nations have achieved independence does not invalidate Fanon's theory. He makes it clear that independence does not translate to authentic freedom and unity of the colonized people. Rather, it is a stepping stone to revolutionary struggles. Satre explains that this struggle is "a work in progress, which begins by the union, in each country, after independences before, of the whole of the colonized people under the command of the peasant class."[60] Although the era of colonialism has elapsed, Africans are being recolonized through productive activities of external imperialists (western bourgeoisie) and African governments. It cannot be rightly gainsaid that the free penetration of imperialists' oligopolies into African nations and their alliance with African governments in this age of mercantilism are responsible for political, social and economic woes of Africans. The phenomena associated with imperialism which include, inter alia, economic and political hegemony, oppressive state machinery, militarism, enslavement and exploitation of indigenous population and racism are intrinsic features of colonialism which Fanon frowns upon and fights against.

A case in point is the violence in the Niger Delta region of Nigeria. Imperialist oligopolies represented by multinational oil companies forge an alliance with the Nigerian State (ruling class) through its agents to mindlessly explore and exploit oil from Niger Delta region. This is done to develop capitalism and maximize profit at all cost without regard to the deplorable state of the environment and the plight of the host communities. It is no longer news that oil spills pollute streams, destroy crops, kill aquatic life of the organisms and make water unsuitable for fishing and unsafe for drinking. Consequently, the natives, who predominantly specialize in farming and fishing, have been denied of their means of livelihood and impoverished. Nwosu laments that "the oil which has brought so much wealth to the multinational oil companies and the Nigerian State has at the same time brought to the people of the Niger Delta untold poverty, disease, persistent pollution, ecological and environmental degradation."[61] Despite the vital contribution of the region to Nigeria's economy, the people have not been adequately compensated and the extent of the development in the region does not commensurate with the level of benefits that accrue from the region.

Piqued by economic deprivation and exploitation, marginalization and developmental neglect, Niger Delta militant youths emerge to struggle for resource control. Rather than involve the armed youths and the community leaders in constructive dialogue and peaceful negotiations, the pattern of regime response is more or less militaristic in nature – unleashing state violence through militarism. The forces that control the Nigerian State (state officials and petrobusiness actors) have privatized the instrumentalities of the state to pursue their private interests "through public works contracts and outright misappropriation of public funds."[62] Thus, the oil exploration and exploitation by the multinational companies have made the region poor, insecure and underdeveloped. In the light of this, Ibeanu notes that Niger Delta is the major source of oil wealth. However, paradoxically, this wealth has created poverty in the region, the national security has generated insecurity in the region, and the national development has underdeveloped the region. The high rate of poverty and underdevelopment in the Niger Delta arising from economic deprivation, injustice and marginalisation is an emblematic of deplorable and socio-economic conditions of the Nigerian society. Needless to say, other parts of the country have their fair share of the political and economic conundrum, hence the agitation of some region for secession.

Another classic case is violence in the northern part of Nigeria. Some analysts usually look at the cause of the persistent spate of militant attacks and killings in the north from political and ethno-religious perspectives. Though the violence and destruction may be motivated and precipitated by political and ethno-religious differences, they have economic undertone. Untold economic hardship in the region arising from poverty and unemployment is the determining factor. Youths have a predisposition towards violence when they suffer from economic deprivation and social alienation. Perpetrators of terrorist acts in Nigeria are mostly hordes of unemployed and hungry youths who are frustrated with their life. An educated gainfully employed person will not abandon the trappings of his work or business and indulge in insurgency or become a slavish stooge for terrorism. There is therefore a strong correlation between poverty and violence. A hungry man is an angry man. When a lot of citizens are poor, hungry and unemployed, insurgency and other crimes ensue.

Besides, the recent atrocious xenophobic violence in South Africa is a consequence of economic deprivation and social alienation of black South Africans. The rage behind the violence unleashed on foreigners (other Africans, particularly Nigerians) is neither xenophobia nor Afrophobia but the high rate of poverty and hunger. The policy of apartheid regime viciously restrains the blacks from achieving parity with their white counterparts by denying them, among other things, access to quality education. Thus, in this post-apartheid society, most black South-African youths lack the requisite skills to compete with the whites for skilled jobs. Regrettably, there is a credibility gap between the promises of post-apartheid governments and their achievements. Despite the promises of the ruling African National Congress (ANC) during campaigns, the blacks are yet to be widely integrated into the socio-political systems. Consequently, the rate of unemployment has surged to 23.5% in South Africa – the worst rate since the first labour force survey in 2008. It is the socio-economic deprivation and alienation that prompt the frustrated and jobless blacks to turn their aggression on the foreigners who are being accused of taking jobs meant for them. Therefore, economic deprivation is the root cause of the violent outbreak. Racism or xenophobia, to use Fanon's terminology, is just the superstructure. Like in the Fanon's colonial world the blacks are conscious that their plight is occasioned by those at the helm of affairs. But they cannot attack their leaders due to adequate security forces in place to ruthlessly suppress any violent outbreak or armed uprising. Thus, they find an outlet for their deep and repressed resentment in violent attacks on other Africans. Racial, tribal and ethnic conflicts, which are reinforced and sustained by exploitative and oppressive colonial rule in Fanon's time, still linger today because decisive social and economic factors in which they are deeply rooted are yet to be completely addressed.

From the foregoing examples, it is obvious that the political and economic activities of the African governments are conditioned for them to accumulate all the resources left by the colonial regime in alliance with the western bourgeoisie, at the expense of the poor masses. Thus, the exploitation, racism, oppression, deprivation and alienation inherent in the Fanon's colonial world persist in African nations.

Concluding Reflections

Fanon has demonstrated that the socio-economic conditions are at the root of the racial problem which engenders the feeling of inferiority complex. He notes that the prevalent racism in the colonial world is deeply rooted in social and economic conditions and so should not be regarded as a mental disturbance. As he puts it: "Racism belongs to the shameless exploitation of one group of men by another which has reached a higher stage of technical development ... The habit of considering racism as a mental quirk, as a psychological flaw must be abandoned."[63] Again, in *Black Skin, White Mask*, he adds that though a psychological interpretation of the black problem is crucial, yet "the effective disalienation of the black man entails an immediate recognition of social and economic realities. If there is an inferiority complex, it is the outcome of a double process: primarily economic; subsequently, the internalization – or, better, epidermalization – of this inferiority."[64]

There is therefore need for restructuring of the existing socio-political systems in African nations which provoke a sense of alienation from the society. Fanon's concern is social freedom – the freedom of the individual in the state. For this freedom to be achieved, it is crucial that the "state not only be free from external control but also that political and social arrangements should be such as to enable man to express and maintain his freedom."[65] It will be a "Pyrrhic victory if the liberation still leaves intact the broad macro structures of economic, political and material conditions that determine everyday existence."[66] Economic exploitation and deprivation violate human dignity. Each individual human being has an intrinsic worth and dignity in virtue of being part of humanity. Social institutions and practices are justified when they promote human dignity. It requires concern and respect for rights equality and justice which are the ultimate preconditions for societal development. It is injustices, oppression and man's inhumanity to man that Fanon frowns upon and fights against.

We must say that though it is the dehumanizing circumstances that prompt Fanon to advocate a violent struggle for liberation, his claim that his call for violence is rooted in "a profound humanism characterized by the primordial concern for the human being and in all human beings, no matter their color and their condition"[67] is untenable. Humanity is indivisible in the sense that no one can degrade or brutalize another without brutalizing himself. In other words, no one can inflict psychic damage on others without inflicting it on himself. This is because when people are dehumanized, their self-worth and dignity are destroyed. In so doing, both the oppressed and oppressor deprive themselves and the world of the benefits of their potential contributions to humanity. Fanon even admits that violence can cause more psychological damage to the psyche of both the colonized people and the colonizers. His psychiatric case histories show that the violence engenders neurosis and distortion of personality.

Besides, Fanon's claim that violent decolonization will create new humanity, unify the people and build solidarity among them leaves much to be desired. Experience and studies have shown that harmony and friendship cannot be secured on the basis of violence, but rather through non-violent struggle which seeks to secure the cooperation of the opponent consistently with truth and justice. Fanon's emphasis on violence risks the reduction of action to reaction, that is, the determination of a solution by the nature of the problem it aims to solve. More often than not, the use of violent resistance is counter-productive and the end for which it is used is defeated. It is not true in reality that violence can be used to quench violence when erupted. "Overtime, the employment of violence has only succeeded in escalating violence."[68] To use violence against violence is to add to the vicious circle of violence, thereby reverting to the Hobbes' state of nature where life is brutish and short. Revolutionary violence does not appeal to humanity and so is undesirable.

Notwithstanding the above-mentioned flaws, Fanon is calling African governments today to nip in the bud the growing racial and ethnic tension across Africa by addressing socio-economic alienation and political injustices which he identifies as the root causes. There is ravaging hunger in Africa and the masses are in dire need of a decent living. The primary duty of any responsible government is the security of lives and property as well as the promotion of people's welfare. Unfortunately, there is a gaping disconnect between African leaders and their masses. We appeal to the African governments to respond to this clarion call by restructuring socio-political systems, developing humans and infrastructure, alleviating poverty, deepening democracy and improving governance.

In the case of Nigeria, there is need for political restructuring of the defective federal system so as to have fair, equitable and balanced federal structure. Currently, there is too much concentration of power at the centre and federating units depend heavily on federal allocations for their needs. True federalism will enable the regions to maximize their potentials, develop at their own pace and contribute their quota to the Federal Government. A nation in turmoil cannot achieve a lasting peace unless they come together to lay down their conditions of political union and reach a compromise. A conference of ethnic nationalities organized by the Jonathan's government in which useful recommendations were made is an effective way of achieving true federalism and peace. Regrettably, the recommendations of the conference have been brushed aside by the present administration.

There is no gain saying the fact that the fight for corruption and security cannot be successfully won, unless the political, social and economic issues are addressed by adopting true federalism. For instance, it is difficult to stem the tide of corruption "where the federating units virtually run on free federal allocations that some people see as national cake, not their own sweet. Conversely, the people will be more vigilant and ready to hold their leaders accountable when the federating units begin to live largely on internally generated revenues and their sweat."[69] Nigerian government must rise to the challenge to resolve the already escalating violent conflict and forestall the future ones before the nation is irretrievably torn apart. Dealing with this despicable act calls for review of the major recommendations of the 2014 National Conference for immediate implementation. Beyond this, there is need to diversify and industrialize the economy, invest in technology and people to drive sustainable economic growth and create jobs.

References

1. E. Hansen, "Freedom and Revolution in the Thought of, Frantz Fanon", *Africa Development/ Afrique et Developpement*, 2, 1 (1977), pp. 18 – 19.
2. F. Fanon, *Toward The African Revolution* trans. by Haakon Chevalier, (New York: Grove Press, 1967), p.53.
3. O. Fashina, "Frantz Fanon and the Ethical Justification of Anti-Colonial Violence", *Social Theory and Practice*, 15, 2 (1989), p. 181.
4. N. Roberts, "Fanon, Satre, Violence and Freedom", *Satre Studies International*, 10, 2 (2004), p. 143.
5. N. Roberts, "Fanon, Satre, Violence and Freedom", 146.
6. N. Roberts, "Fanon, Satre, Violence and Freedom", 146.
7. F. Fanon, *Black Skin, White Masks*, trans. by Charles Lam Markmann, (New York: Grove Press, 1967), p. 202.
8. F. Fanon, *The Wretched of the Earth*, trans. by Constance Farrington, (New York: Grove Press, 1963), p. 35.
9. F. Fanon, *The Wretched of the Earth*, 37.
10. E. Hansen, "Freedom and Revolution in the Thought of, Frantz Fanon", 25.
11. Satre, "Preface to the Wretched of the Earth", 14.
12. E. Hansen, "Freedom and Revolution in the Thought of, Frantz Fanon", 25.
13. Satre, "Preface to the Wretched of the Earth", 14.
14. M. Kebede, "The Rehabilitation of Violence and the Violence of Rehabilitation", *Journal of Black Studies*, 31, 5(2001), p. 540.
15. Fanon, "The Wretched of the Earth", 39.
16. A. Césaire, quoted by Dennis Forsythe in "Frantz Fanon: Black Theoretician", *The Black Scholar*, 1, 5, (1970), p.6.
17. Satre, "Preface to the Wretched of the Earth", 16.
18. Fanon, "The Wretched of the Earth", 51.
19. Fanon, "The Wretched of the Earth", 53.
20. Satre, "Preface to the Wretched of the Earth", 17 – 18.
21. D. Wright, "Fanon and Africa: A Retrospect", *The Journal of Modern African Studies*, 24, 4 (1986), p. 683.
22. Fanon, "The Wretched of the Earth", 6.
23. Fanon, "The Wretched of the Earth", 59.

24. Fanon, "The Wretched of the Earth", 58 – 59.
25. Fanon, "The Wretched of the Earth", 71.
26. Fanon, "The Wretched of the Earth", 70.
27. F. Fanon, quoted by Emmanuel Hansen in "Frantz Fanon: Portrait of a Revolutionary Intellectual", *Transition*, No. 46 (1974), p. 31.
28. Fanon, "Toward the African Revolution", 64.
29. F. Fanon, quoted by Emmanuel Hansen in "Frantiz Fanon: Portrait of a Revolutionary Intellectual", p. 31.
30. Fanon, "The Wretched of the Earth", 60.
31. Fanon, "The Wretched of the Earth", 33.
32. Fanon, "The Wretched of the Earth", 35.
33. Fanon, "The Wretched of the Earth", 49 – 50.
34. J.P. Satre, *Critique of Dialectical Reason*, (London: NLB, 1979), p. 803.
35. R. Bernasconi, "The Wretched of the Earth as the Fulfillment of Satre's Critique of Dialectical reason, *Satre Studies International*, 16, 2 (2010), p. 39.
36. Fanon, "The Wretched of the Earth", 87.
37. Satre, "Preface to the Wretched of the Earth", 20.
38. O. Fashina, p. 186.
39. Fanon, "The Wretched of the Earth", 93.
40. Fanon, 187.
41. Fanon, "The Wretched of the Earth", 93.
42. C.E. Butterworth and I.L. Gendzier, "A Review of Frantz Fanon and the Justice of Violence: An Essay on Irene L. Gendzier's Frantz: A Critical Study", *Middle East Journal*, 28, 4 (1974), p. 455.
43. Fanon, "The Wretched of the Earth", 72.
44. J. Penny, "Passing into the Universal: Fanon, Satre and the Colonial Dialectic", *Paragraph*, 27, 3 (2004), p. 53.
45. O. Fashina, "Frantz Fanon and the Ethical Justification of Anti-Colonial Violence", p. 184.
46. Fanon, "The Wretched of the Earth", 43.
47. Fanon, "The Wretched of the Earth", 46.
48. Fanon, "The Wretched of the Earth", 92.
49. Fanon, "The Wretched of the Earth", 92.
50. Fanon, "The Wretched of the Earth", 93.
51. B.K. Jha, "Fanon's Theory of Violence: A Critique" *The Indian Journal of Political Science*, 49, 3 (1988), p. 363.
52. Fanon, "The Wretched of the Earth", 85.
53. L.S. Senghor, *Negritude: A Humanism of the Twentieth Century*, (New York: Vintage, 1970), p. 179.
54. Fanon, "Black Skin, White Masks", 226.
55. Fanon, "The Wretched of the Earth", 229 – 230.
56. Fanon, "The Wretched of the Earth", 17.
57. E. Hansen, "Freedom and Revolution in the Thought of, Frantz Fanon", 32.
58. E. Hansen, "Freedom and Revolution in the Thought of, Frantz Fanon", 32.

59. E. Hansen, "Freedom and Revolution in the Thought of, Frantz Fanon", 33.

60. Satre, "Preface to the Wretched of the Earth", 10.

61. I.J.D. Nwosu, "Marginality and the Niger Delta Crises: Ogoni, Ijaw and Warri Crises in Perspectives" In *Peace Studies and Conflict Resolution in Nigeria: A reader*, ed. by M. Ikejiani-Clark, (Ibadan: Spectrum Books Ltd, 2009), p. 546.

62. O. Ibeanu, *Affluence and Affliction: The Niger Delta as a Critique of Political Science in Nigeria*. 2008 Inaugural Lecture, University of Nigeria Nsukka, (Nsukka: University of Nigeria Senate Ceremonials Committee, 2008), p. 22.

63. Fanon, "Toward the African Revolution", 37 – 38.

64. Fanon, "Black Skin, White Mask", 11.

65. E. Hansen, "Freedom and Revolution in the Thought of, Frantz Fanon", 25.

66. G.F. Sefa and M. Simmons, "The Pedagogy of Fanon: An Introduction", *Counterpoints*, Vol. 38 (2010), p. xvii.

67. F. Fanon, quoted by Oladipo Fashina in "Frantz Fanon and the Ethical Justification of Anti-Colonial Violence", p. 198.

68. A. Akpuru-Aja, *Basic Concepts, Issues and Strategies of Peace and Conflict Resolution*, (Enugu: Keny and Brothers Ent., 2007), p. 112.

69. I. Ekweremadu, "Only Restructuring Can Save Nigeria" July 2016, http://politics.naij.com/897423-finally-ekweremadu-dares-buhari-words.html (Accessed 24 April, 2017.)

CHAPTER TWELVE

IGWEBUIKE AS A HERMENEUTIC OF INDIVIDUALITY AND COMMUNALITY IN AFRICAN ONTOLOGY

KANU, Ikechukwu Anthony

Executive Summary

One of the allegations against African philosophy and acting is that of collectivism, which excludes individuality in the African universe. The present work on schedule responds to this allegation by attempting to prove that there is individuality in the African communal universe. This is achieved by relying on Igwebuike philosophy taken from the Igbo-African socio-cultural background. The Igbo concept of the self was studied to see how in differentiating the self from the other in Igbo ontology, individuality and identity is unveiled. It further studies the use of personal pronouns and names in Igbo ontology to reveal how the Igbo express the individuality of persons in the community. The Igbo philosophy of the body was employed as an instrument of personal identity to show how, through the body, the Igbo-African differentiates individual persons from others in the community. Finally, the concept of Chi, which is an Igbo principle of individuation for the interpretation of personal historical and religious experiences, was studied to see how the particular is not lost in the universal. The phenomenological and hermeneutic methods were employed for this research. This paper submits that in the African universe, while the ontology of the person is founded on the particularity of the individual, implying that it is the metaphysics of the particular that founds identity, it is the community that gives meaning to such an existence and grounds such an identity.

Keywords: Igwebuike, Self, African, Philosophy, Individuality, Communality.

Introduction

African thought, philosophy and ethics have been accused by both Western and African scholars of swallowing up the individual and his or her personal identity in the community oriented pattern of thinking. This perspective is the product of an interpretation of the African way of life, which is community focused and reinforced by the African's cultural orientation characterized by love, brotherhood, concern for the other and a sense of belonging to the community. The community has set laws which members follow for the purpose of order and the preservation of the community. From the foregoing, it would look to a distant observer that everyone acts, thinks and behaves in the same way. According to Edeh (1983):

> From this, it would seem that by living in such a community, the lucidity of one's self-consciousness is veiled and therefore one is not yet in a completely realized communication since one is not yet aware of autonomous selfhood or will. In such a community, it could appear as if each person is reduced to an ego point which is substitutable for another mere ego point. (pp. 135-136).

In the midst of the questioning of the quality of the individuality of the African individual within the context of the community, this work makes an attempt to study the African concept of the self as it relates to the community against the background of Igwebuike philosophy. Igwebuike philosophy has been developed from the Igbo background. It is a principle that is at the heart of African thought, and in fact, the modality of being in African ontology. Igwebuike is a composite word made up of three dimensions (Kanu 2015). Therefore, it can be employed as a word or used as a sentence: as a word, it is written as *Igwebuike*, and as a sentence, it is written as, *Igwe bu ike*, with the component words enjoying some independence in terms of space. The three words involved: *Igwe* is a noun which means number or population, usually a huge number or population. *Bu* is a verb, which means *is*. *Ike* is another verb, which means *strength* or *power* (Kanu 2016). Thus, put together, it means 'number is strength' or 'number is power', that is, when human beings come together in solidarity and complementarity, they are powerful or can constitute an insurmountable force (Kanu, 2017). Its English equivalents are 'complementarity', 'solidarity' and 'harmony'. The preferred concept, however, is 'complementarity'. From this philosophical background, questions such as these would be responded to: Is the African an individual person who is capable of deciding on his own what to do and what not to do or is he a lump of persons who act in a chorus? Is the African capable of individuality or is he locked up in communalism? This is the burden looming at the horizon of this piece. It would, therefore, study the African concept of the self, names, personal pronouns, *Chi* principle and the human body to see if there is the possibility of a simple individuation and identity within the complexity of the community.

Cartesian Conceptualization of the Self

An attempt to understand the conceptualization of the self within the context of Igwebuike philosophy would be best appreciated against a different background. And the different background that would be of concern here is the western conceptualization scheme of the person, which is expressed in the Cartesian concept of the self. The Cartesian concept of the self without the other can be traced back to the medieval ages.

Boethius (480 AD) in his *De Persona et Duabus Naturis,* held that a person is an 'individual substance of a rational nature' (*persona est rationalis naturae individual substantia*). This later became the classical definition of person. St Thomas Aquinas (1224 AD) after Boethius, in his *Summa Theologica,* defines a person as the *subsistens rationale* (a rational subsistent). According to Okon (2010), Thomas Aquinas' concept of a person implies:

a. A person is a substance not accident.
b. A person must have a complete nature, and so that which lacks completeness and remains only a part of nature does not satisfy this definition.
c. It is subsistent by itself, the person exists in himself and for himself, being the ultimate subject possessor of his nature and all his acts and so is the ultimate subject of predication of all its attributes.
d. It is separated from others.
e. It is of a rational nature, this excludes all supposits that lack rationality.

This notwithstanding, with Rene Descartes (1596-1650 AD), philosophy started a new way, that of gnoseology. He defines the person in relation to self-consciousness. In the *Second Meditation,* Descartes (1637), through his methodical doubt, discovers that something resists doubt. That is, the fact that it is he who doubts, and who can be deceived. He thus, arrives at *Cogito ergo sum* (I think therefore, I am). To the question, who am I? Descartes answers simply, a "thinking thing", a thing that essentially has mental experiences. Descartes' transformation of the person from an ontological to a psychological fact, opened the door to a series of either great diminutions or of enormous exaggerations of the concept of person. Since the time of Descartes, individual consciousness has been taken as the privileged centre of identity, while 'the other' is seen as an epistemological problem, or as an inferior, reduced or negated form of the same. The self in the Cartesian scheme sees itself without the other (Kanu 2016 and 2017). This perspective has influenced western philosophy.

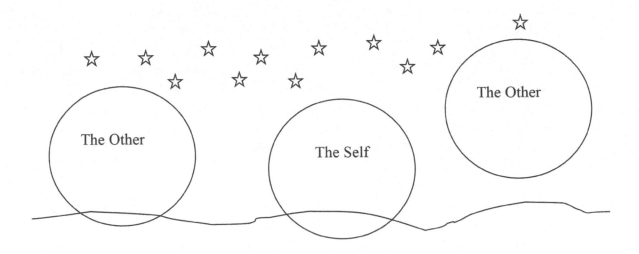

FIGURE 1: **The Self In Relation to the other in Western Conceptualization Scheme**

The study of the historical development of Western philosophy and the evolution of African thought, unveils an obvious diversity between the Western conceptualization scheme and the African conception of reality. From the Cartesian model, Onyeocha (1997) and (2006) points out that while the Western pattern of thought is exclusivistic, depersonalized, objectivised and more concerned with analysis; the African scheme of conceptualization is inclusivistic, integrative, non-reductionistic, concrete, personalized and subjectivised in all its manifestations, expressing the interconnectedness of reality- a world of relationship, harmony, continuality and complementarity. The dualistic and exclusivistic Western perception of reality understands a person in relation to the other in terms of *"I and Not-I"*. This creates a dichotomy that brings in a strong divide between the *"I* and the other", which could set groups and individuals against themselves.

The Problem of Collectivism and Unanimism in African

Philosophy

While individualism defines the Western conceptualization scheme, African philosophy has been criticized on the grounds of collectivism and unanimism as regards the self in relation to the other. It is argued that while Western philosophy is the record of the philosophies of individual persons, for instance, we have Thales, Anaximander, Anaximenes, Pythagoras, Empedocles, Heraclitus, Socrates, Plato, Aristotle, St Augustine, St Thomas Aquinas, Descartes, Locke, Hegel, Russell, Whitehead, Rawls, Rorty etc., in African philosophy, it is different. Afolayan (2006) writes that "Instead of the gallery of individual philosophers who symbolize the cultures confrontation with its experiences, ... there is an attempt to summarize the philosophical enterprise in Africa into a collective, communal framework" (p. 22).

Appiah (1992) puts the blame of unanimism on oral tradition. He writes, "Oral tradition has a habit of only transmitting consensus" (p.92). based on the collective character of African philosophy, Hountondji (1976) described African philosophy as simply a myth, the myth of unanimity and consensus. It is not surprising that he rejects concepts such as Igbo philosophy, Akan philosophy, Bantou philosophy or Dogon philosophy. Reacting to Hountondji's perspective, Gyekye (1987) accuses him of denigrating, if not ignoring:

> ...the relevance and impact of the culture on the reflections of the individual thinker. Believing, as they do, that philosophizing is a wholly individualistic affair, they fail to recognize that the thinker perforce operates on the diffuse and inchoate ideas of the cultural milieu. We obviously cannot divorce the philosophy of an individual thinker from the ideas current among the people, for the philosophy of the individual thinker is rooted in the beliefs and assumptions of the culture. (p. 25).

While it is accepted as true that African philosophy, in the past, is collective, it is also good to mention that its collective character does not mean that it ceases to be philosophy or critical. Gyekye (1987) argues that, "In Africa's historical past, there has been an absence of ... known and identifiable individual thinkers who stand out and can claim to have originated specific philosophical doctrines and to whom we can trace such doctrines" (p. 24). But this is not to say that there were no individual thinkers, for that they are not known does not mean that they did not exist. He goes on to write:

> But surely, it was individual wise men who created African 'collective' philosophy. A particular thought or idea is, as regards its genesis, the product of an individual mind. And although it is logically possible for two or more individuals to think the same thought or to have the same idea at the same time, nevertheless, the production of the thought as such is the work of the mind of each of the individuals concerned. It is always an individual's idea or thought or proposition that is accepted and gains currency among other people; at this stage, however, it is erroneously assumed to be the collective thought of the people. (p. 24).

Although African philosophy is regarded as a collective philosophy, they were borne from individual minds, and although we regard the philosophy of the West as composed of individual thinkers, they were furnished with the ideas, beliefs and thoughts of their society. Explaining why they are referred to as Oriental philosophy, speaking of the Oriental mind, British philosophy, speaking of the British Mind, European philosophy, speaking of the European mind, German philosophy, speaking of the German mind, etc.

The Self and the Conceptualization of Individuality

In the Igbo expression of a person, we discover that a person is an identity. In reference to a person, it is said *onye mmadu*. Moreso, the use of pronouns by the Igbo, like *Mmu* (I), *Ngi* (You), *Nginwa* (Yourself), *Nmunwa* (Myself), *Nyanwa* (Himself, Herself), show that a person is conceived with an identity, a primary statement of reality and not mixed up with others without an identity. The attachment *nwa* is a demonstrative which means 'this here'. Thus, *mmunwa*would literally mean 'Myself here'; *Nginwa* 'Yourself here'. It is an emphatic pronoun. The word which the Igbo uses to speak of the self is *onwe,* and so the Igbo can talk of *onwe gi* 'yourself', *onwe ha* 'Themselves', *onwe m,* 'Myself', *onwe ya* 'Himself or herself'. The original root of the word *onwe*can be traced back to *nwe* that means 'to own'. Thus, *onwe gi,* would mean he that owns himself, *onwe ya,* would mean he or she that owns himself or herself. The idea of ownership over the self introduces the idea of independence from the other. The *onwe,* therefore, becomes the source of identity of the individual. According to Okere (2015), the *onwe:*

> is not describable and has no name and function except as the ultimate author of all the functions of the individual, the carrier of all experience. It is the link between the experiences of yesterday and today, the basis of that proprietorship by which these fleeting multitudes of experience are one and are mine. (pp. 163-164).

The *onwe*is, therefore, at the centre of human action and engagements. No one can speak of the *onwe* in a way that denotes distance or as a part of him or her. For the *onwe* is not a part of the person as one can speak of the hands or legs or ears. The *onwe* is yourself in its totality. While the *onwe* conveys the reality of identity and alterity, 'I' different from the 'Other', it is also a basic indication of personal autonomy. Personal autonomy brings in the idea of freedom, for he who is autonomous is free. Thus, the Igbo-African is free because he is autonomous. If the *onwe* is autonomous in the community of the others, it is obvious that the Igbo-African has an individuality even in the midst of communality.

Personal Names/Pronouns and Individuality

Personal names in African ontology recognizes personal identity. It is in fact the first mark of personal identity in African communities. Once a child is born, he is given an identity as *Chukwuma, Chukwuka, Onyema, Adaku, Ikechukwu, Adaora, uchenna, Emeka, Chiugo, Nnennia.* The peculiarity of the circumstances leading to the birth of persons affects to a great extent the kind of name that is given to the person. Even when people are born under the same circumstance and given the same name, their names are particular to them and do not have the same meaning-as it is unique to them. Tempels (1959) avers that "The first criterion is the name. The name expresses the individual character of the being. The name is not a simple external courtesy; it is the very reality of the individual" (p. 106).Bujo (1998)asserts that "For many African people, the name is not a mere ritual which defends and protects the person, but is the bearer of an action and a message. In a specific manner, it contains a whole programme for life, which everybody has to realize individually" (p. 147). Names carry the history and prehistory of individuals, families and communities. Thus, a name(s) for the Igbo is very important for his identity, and that is why he says *afamefuna*- let my name not demise. This is because the demise of his name is the demise of his identity. This is why every Igbo-African works hard to achieve something in the community so that his name does not demise. This makes a strong connection between the name and the person. Mbiti (1970) posits that the name is the person, and many names are often descriptive of the individual, particularly names acquired as the person grows. The reference to personal names points to the fact that in Africa people were viewed as persons and not just in the collective as a community. If people were viewed collectively then there would be no need for a name.

The Body as an Indication of Individuality

The body in Igbo language is *ahu*. Etymologically, it can be traced to the Igbo word- *hu*, which means 'to see'. In relation to *ahu,* it means that the body is that part of the self which can be seen, it is visible, seeable, tangible. When a child is born, his *ahu* helps people around him in identifying him. When a person has polio, the sight of him and the nature of his *ahu* helps a person to identify him. When an ancestor reincarnates, sometimes the *ahu* helps the family into which the child has been born to identify the ancestor who has returned. For instance, in cases of an ancestor who lost his five fingers while he lived, and when a child is born after his death and the child is born without five fingers, even before divination, it is believed that it is the ancestor that has returned. And in most cases the divination confirms it. In a situation of this kind the child could be named *Ahunna,* that is, the father's body, if it is the father who has reincarnated in him. Thus, the *ahu* helps in identifying a person as an individual who is different from the other. It must be noted that, although the *ahu* occupies a very important place in identifying a person, the *ahu* is not the self, but an outward expression of the self. It is through the *ahu* that the self is known and expressed. In relation to the individuality of each person, every *ahu* is unique. There are no two *ahu* that are the same. Each person has his or her own *ahu* which differentiates him or her from the others.

Personal Chi as an Indication of Individuality

The Igbo believes in the existence of a personal guardian, protector or divine double conceived as a part of God in man or the divine part of man appointed by God to watch over the individual person as he or she fulfils his or her personal destiny. It is called a divine double because while it is resident in the individual person, it deputizes for *Chineke* or *Chukwu.* As a divine force, agent or power, it is unique to the individual person, and part and constitutive of the individual person. There can't be one same *Chi* for two persons. The Chi is not the self, neither is it the soul or the spirit of a person. For if it were the self or the soul or the spirit of a person then the self cannot pray to it, for that would mean the self-praying or honoring the self. Beyond the fact that it is a principle for explaining historical and religious experiences, the *Chi* according to Okere (2015):

> Is also part of the individual's identity and is seen as the prime moving force and principle of individualism in Igbo culture. As such, it is strictly personal, indivisible, not shared or sharable with others as the Igbo says: *(out)?nne namu mana owughi otu chi neke:* same mother but different *Chi,* that is, a person has the same mother as his sibling but his *Chi* is strictly his. (p. 167).

From the foregoing, *Chi* becomes an instrument of individuation and a characteristic attribute of individual persons. It is the principle of destiny- and just as everyone has his own destiny, everyone also has his own *Chi*.

The Problem of Individuality and Community: An Igwebuike Response

Having established the uniqueness and individuality of each person, Igwebuike philosophy understands individuality not as the antithesis of community but as a basis for relationship in the community. Therefore, the oneness and personess in a person is what makes him or her to relate to the other. If all realities were one reality, then there would be no relationship, but the fact that the African world is one that is complementary and relational indicates that there are individual persons that relate. Ezekwonna (2005) posits that: "The community recognizes this personhood and knows that 'I' cannot be 'you' and that 'you' can only relate to 'I' in other for them to achieve their goals and those of the community" (p. 64). Despite the community influence, each person maintains his or her identity, however, it is through relationship in the community that a person's personhood becomes clearer and developed: through constant contact with the other person, your personality learns and is influenced. The African individual person is a social being and not a solitary being. Nzomiwu (1999) expresses this thus:

> For personality, having its root in spirit rather than in matter expresses itself primarily in love, which involves the power to give oneself and to receive the gift of another. Personality emphasizes community for it is dynamic out-going passes properly to a trait of an African person. (p. 19).

How does a person's personality develop through interaction with other persons? As an individual person, no one is self-sufficient. The goods in us are developed when we interact with other people. The entire cultural life is imparted through relationship with the other. Thus, in African ontology, the conceptualization of a person includes the person's dialogical relationship with his environment. There is no individual person without a world, and this world is the sociality and materiality that defines his personhood. For it is in the process of asserting himself in the community that the intelligibility of a person's autonomous choices of goals and plans for his life becomes crystal clear. To disassociate oneself from the community is to weaken the personhood of a person and, therefore, the being of the community.

From the foregoing, Igwebuike is not a philosophy of collectivism. It recognizes the particular which complements the other. And its recognition of the particular is closely linked to its respect for individuality. It is, therefore, neither collectivism nor individualism. Igwebuike, thus, contradicts the Cartesian conceptualization of the individual in terms of which the individual can be conceived without necessarily conceiving the other person. Manda (2015) avers that in the Cartesian self, the individual exists prior to, or separately or independently of the other or others in the community of people. Therefore, the remaining part of the society outside of the self is conceived as a nothing but an added extra to a pre-existent and self-sufficient being. This perspective exaggerates the solitary aspect of the person or individual to the detriment of the community. In Descarte's *corgito ergo sum*we find an individualism that is not the opposite of Igwebuike, but rather the opposite of collectivism, which is different in nuance from Igwebuike. Thus, the opponent of individualism becomes collectivism. Below is an attempt to present in a diagram the relationship between the self and the other in Igwebuike philosophy.

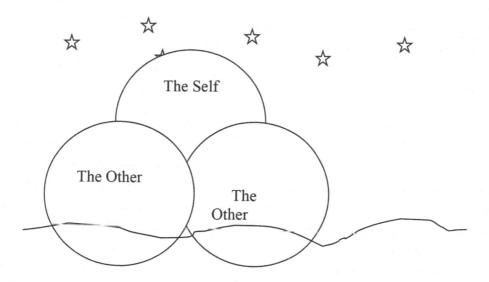

FIGURE 2: **The Self In Relation to the other in Igwebuike Conceptualization Scheme**

Igwebuike is distanced from collectivism because in collectivism, the individual vanishes in the community without any relevance. This was the impression that Gyekye wanted to correct when he responded to the interpretation of African thought by Hountondji. Gyekye (1987) understands the idea of collective thought as employed by Hountondji as a misnomer. He writes:

> There is, strictly speaking, no such thing as collective thought, if this means that ideas result from the intellectual production of a whole collectivity. What has come to be described a collective thought is nothing but the ideas of individual wise people; individual ideas that, due to lack of doxographic tradition in Africa, became part of the pool of communal thought, resulting in the obliteration of differences among these ideas, and in the impression that traditional thought was a monolithic system that does not allow for divergent ideas. (p. 24).

Igwebuike understands persons as individuals, however, in a community, and in terms of their relationship with others. Although persons are first individuals, in African ontology they conceptualize themselves only in relation to the other. In this case, individuals only exist in terms of their relationship with other people or individuals. The individual is a person who corresponds to the multiplicity of relationships in the community. This pushes the Cartesian *corgito ergo sum* into a more complex reality, from an understanding of the individual as a solitary reality to a reality in solidarity, from an independent reality to an interdependent reality, from individuality in contrast to community to an individual in the community, from an individual filled with a sense of solitariness to an individual filled with a sense of the other. Igwebuike is based on the nature of the African universe which is complementary and relational in character.

Conclusion

The foregoing has studied the possibility of individuality in the African communitarian universe. It began from the Cartesian conceptualization of the self- the *corgito ergo sum*, typical of the Western perspective of the self as the fundamental western conceptualization of the self- that is, individualism. It further studied the alleged crisis of collectivism in African philosophy and the attempt by Gyekye to debunk the idea of collectivism in African philosophy. For a more profound study of the problem at hand- the dynamics of individuality and communality, the Igbo-African background is relied upon, since Igwebuike philosophy is itself an Igbo philosophy. And to prove that there is still individuality even in the presence of communality, the concept of the self in Igbo ontology is studied to see how in differentiating the self from the other in Igbo ontology, individuality and identity is emphasized. It further studied the use of names in Igbo ontology to reveal how the Igbo expresses the individuality of each individual. The Igbo philosophy of the body is also employed as an instrument of personal identity to show how, through names, the Igbo-African differentiates individual persons from others in the community. Finally, the concept *Chi* which is an Igbo principle of individuation for the interpretation of personal historical and religious experiences was studied to see how the individual ontologically is not mixed up with the other.

As a study in Igwebuike philosophy, this piece has shown that, although in African philosophy there is communality of people, the communality of people has not degenerated into communalism. Every sense of communality perceived in the African universe is a product of individuality, for unless there are individuals, there cannot be a community. The beauty of the African universe is the presence of an individuality that relates freely and without losing their individuality in a community.

References

Afolayan, A. (2006). Some Methodological Issues in the History of African Philosophy. In O. Oladipo (Ed.). *Core Issues in African Philosophy* (pp. 21-40). Ibadan: Hope.

Appiah, K. A. (1992). *In my father's House: Africa in the Philosophy of Culture.* New York: Oxford University Press.

Bujo, B. (1998). *The Ethical Dimension of Community.* Nairobi: Paulines.

Descartes, R. (1983). *Discourse on method and the meditations.* Trans. John Vietch. London: Penguin Classics.

Edeh, E. (1983). *Towards Igbo metaphysics* Chicago: Loyola University Press.

Ezekwonna, F. C. (2005). *African communitarian ethic: The basis for the moral conscience and autonomy of the individual. Igbo culture as a case study.* Peter Lang: Germany.

Gyekye, K. (1987). *An essay on African philosophical thought: The Akan conceptual scheme*. Cambridge: Cambridge University Press.

Hountondji, P. J. (1976). *African philosophy: Myth and reality*. Indianapolis: Indiana University Press.

Kanu, I. A. (2015a). *A hermeneutic approach to African Traditional Religion, theology and philosophy*. Augustinian: Nigeria.

Kanu, I. A. (2016). *Igwebuike as an Igbo-African Response to the Problem of Personal Identity and Alterity*. A paper presented at the 14th Annual Conference of the Igbo Studies Association, held at the Dominican University, River Forest, Illinois, USA, from May 12th to 14th.

Kanu, I. A. (2017). *African Philosophy, Globalisation and the Priority of Otherness*. A paper presented at the 2017 Philosophy Week of Saint Thomas Aquinas Major Seminary, Makurdi, Benue State Chapter of the Nigerian Major Seminaries Association of Philosophy Students. On 13th May.

Manda, D. S. (2015). *Ubuntu philosophy as an African philosophy for peace*. Retrieved 10/6/17 from www.africanfiles.org/article.asp?ID=20361.

Mbiti, J. S. (1970). *African religions and philosophy*. Nairobi: East African Educational Publishers.

Nzomiwu, J. P. (1999). *The concept of justice among the traditional Igbo: An ethical inquiry*. Awka: Fab.

Okere, T. (2015). *The hermeneutics of philosophy, religion and culture*. J. O. Oguejiofor (Ed.), A. C. Onuorah (Comp.). Colour Print Group: USA.

Okon, J. A. (2010). Rethinking the idea of human personhood. In M. F. Asiegbu and J. C. Chukwuokolo (Eds.). *Personhood and personal identity: A philosophical study*. Enugu: SNAAP.

Tempels, P. (1959). *Bantu Philosophy*. Paris: Presence Africaine.

ABOUT THE AUTHOR

Ikechukwu Anthony KANU, O.S.A is a Friar of the Order of Saint Augustine, Province of Nigeria. He is Professor of African Philosophy and Religion, Tansian University, and a Tenured Professor of Orthodox Studies at The University of America, San Francisco, USA. The former Rector of Villanova Polytechnic, Imesi Ile, Osun State and currently an Adjunct Professor to the University of Jos, Plateau State, Veritas University Abuja and Saint Albert the Great Major Seminary, Abeokuta. He is the President of the Association for the Promotion of African Studies (APAS) and the Global President of the World Cultural Studies Research Association (WCRA).

Printed in the United States
by Baker & Taylor Publisher Services